CLIPS THAT Move MOUNTAINS

2ND EDITION

DR. PATTY SADALLAH

Copyright © 2019 by Dr. Patty Sadallah

Clips that Move Mountains
2nd *Edition*
by Dr. Patty Sadallah

Printed in the United States of America

ISBN 9780999282328

All rights reserved solely by the author. The author guarantees all contents are original and do not infringe upon the legal rights of any other person or work. No part of this book may be reproduced in any form without the permission of the author. The views expressed in this book are not necessarily those of the publisher.

Clips that Move Mountains: QR Code Edition was published ©2013

Unless otherwise indicated, Bible quotations are taken from the New International Version (NIV). Copyright © 2012 by Zondervan.

Published by IngramSpark

CLIPS THAT *Move* MOUNTAINS

2ND EDITION

DR. PATTY SADALLAH

IngramSpark

Dedication

To the Lord Jesus Christ who saved me, refines me, empowers me and emboldened me to write this book. And to the many reader/viewers: may you bless multitudes with your kingdom impact.

"You did not choose me, but I chose you and appointed you so that you might go and bear fruit—fruit that will last—and so that whatever you ask in my name, the Father will give you." ~ John 15:16

Table of Contents

Acknowledgements xi
What's New in the 2nd Edition? xiii
BACK STORY & INSTRUCTIONS 1
    What is Clips that Move Mountains? 2
    God's MUCH bigger vision 3
    About the Movie Clips 4
    Clip Instructions 5
    Clip Disclaimer 6
LOVE, MIRACLES & IMPACT 9
    The Beginning of my Love Story 9
    Miracles are Signs of God's Love and Power 16
    Pray for Rain- Clip from Faith like Potatoes 18
    Ordinary People/Extraordinary Impact 22
    God's One Big Plan: Strangers clip 23
    Your Promised Land & The Territory of
    Christian Impact Model 26
    Discipleship 33
    Life Application: LOVE, MIRACLES & IMPACT 35

BEGIN CENTER: Choose Jesus 37
Why Choose Jesus? Prophetic Proof Clip 40

Do your Homework 44

You Need HIM: Clip from Fireproof 48

Free Ticket 51

What the Father Did for You: Clip from
Most- The Bridge 56

Salvation Prayer 62

Life Application: BEGIN CENTER 64

NORTH: Grow Your Relationship with Christ 65
The Bible- God's Love Story & Mouthpiece 65

Identity in Christ: Identity Clip 68

What Jesus had to say about the mustard seed: 72

The Praise Alphabet 74

Pray for Shrimp: Clip from Forrest Gump 76

Discerning God's Will 78

Really P.R.A.Y.: The Skinny on Prayer Clip 82

Buh Bye Lymes and other Prayer Miracles 88

Life Application: NORTH 100

WEST: Overcoming Life's Challenges and Finding Forgiveness 103
It's not a dead end ... Clip 1 from Unconditional 107

No Storm Can Take the Son Away – Clip 2
from Unconditional 110

Slingshot Faith 111

Getting to Forgiveness: Clip from October Baby 112

Table of Contents

Dad's Transformation Clip from Undaunted: The Early Life of Josh McDowell.. 115

How to Set the Captive Free 117

What if the one you need to forgive is you?...................... 121

What if the one you need to forgive is God?..................... 123

Life Application: WEST.. 127

SOUTH: Leveraging Life Circumstances to Share your Faith and Light.......................................129

Truth 130

Lead People to the Truth- Clip 1 from King's Faith..... 137

Live out the Truth- Clip 2 from Kings Faith 139

Put on the Full Armor of God.. 140

Ready Yourself to Share the Truth- Clip from Seklas Seeds 143

How to Follow God's Lead: God Speaks Clip 149

The Romans Road... 157

Be the Moon 158

Life Application: SOUTH 160

EAST: Use your Gifts to Bless Others & Advance the Kingdom 163

Work is Worship Clip 164

He can use you too 168

Don't limit God.. 170

Prepare your Fields: Clip from Facing the Giants 174

The Potter and His Clay: Clip from Surf's Up................. 178

Spiritual Gifts and Finding Your Calling............................ 181

    Manifestation Gifts 184

    Ministry Gifts 189

    Motivational Gifts 192

    BHAGS.. 199

    Future Vision 202

    Life Application: EAST 206

BACK TO CENTER: Living the Abundant Christian Life ..209

    Begin Center- Choose Jesus... 209

    How will you be remembered? Legacy Clip 212

    The Crowns: Eternal Rewards... 216

    Plant the Seed: Clip from The Lorax 220

    Unless… 222

    Do Something 223

    Shine Your Light Clip 224

    Life Application: Back to Center... 227

About the Author **229**
Featured Filmmakers and Other Partners **231**
Other Books by: Dr. Patty Sadallah **239**
End Notes..**241**

Acknowledgements

I would like to thank my prayer partners in this project; Katie Beckwith, Mike Noble, Dr. Anthony "Doc" Raimondo, Larry Silver and Becky Difillipo and all the members of the School of the Spirit who have been faithfully encouraging me all these years and who prayed with me regularly for this project and all other needs.

I would also like to thank Annelie and Roger Rudlaff for help and ongoing support in finding clips from Christian Film Database and their website www.ChristianFilmDatabase.com. I would also like to thank my daughter Jamael Szucs who edited both versions of this book and Tracy Briggs, Pastor John Guenther for editing assistance in the original version.

I would like to thank Jim Kilgore, Gretchen Donahue, Charisse and Perry Anderson, Jeanette Chamberlin, Pete Formica, George Simon, Lisa Ryan and in memory of my mother, Norma MacInnis, for financial support and prayers.

Thank you to Scott Douglass for the wonderful work on the book trailer and for my daughter Leah Sadallah who connected me with his company www.FixThisinPost.com. Thanks also to my daughter Noelle Sadallah who played trombone in the piece used for the trailer.

I appreciate the Jenkins Group and the Illumination Awards reviewers for honoring me with a Gold Medal for this book in the Enduring Light Christian Insight category. And for Rachel Jones with her marketing assistance. Thanks also to Matias Baldanza who designed this book cover through www.fiverr.com

Love and thanks to my husband George Sadallah who prays with me daily and my wonderful children Leah, Noelle and Jamael and her husband Nick, and my mother-in-law, Jennie Sadallah, whose love and support helped me write this book one day at a time. And most importantly, thank you Lord for giving me this blessed assignment and equipping me to finish it. To God be the Glory!

What's New in the 2nd Edition?

*I*n the 6 years since the original publishing of this book as a QR Code Edition, the Lord has taken me on quite the journey. A year after the original Clips book was released, *Journey to the Abundant Christian Life,* a Bible study companion book to Clips was published. A couple of years after that, I knew that I was supposed to write more books, and even knew in my spirit that the next book was supposed to be about the Names and Promises of God, but really didn't know how to go about it.

Serendipitously, the Lord led me to Christian Leadership University to pursue a Doctorate in Discipleship and put me on the path of one of the most incredible educational experiences I would never have imagined as possible. CLU is unique in that it is the only university that focuses on hearing God's voice and teaching the tools of Jesus encounter to such a degree that He becomes your personal Teacher.

The coursework and subsequent dissertation project led to the publication of *How to Live a Worry- Free Life: Just Ask Jesus Series Book 1*. This book teaches the tools of direct Jesus encounter along with showing how finding the Names, Promises of God as wells as the conditions of promises and how to pray them with authority. These lessons are the secrets to living a worry-free life. This book does not go into those steps, but some of the lessons that were learned through that Doctoral journey along with actual conversations and adventures with Jesus are peppered throughout this Second Edition. *How to Find your Calling: Just Ask Jesus Series Book 2* is nearly finished and will be coming out in 2019.

The first version of this paperback book was a QR Code Edition. This version only includes the QR code for the cover trailer. For those who know what to do, they can use their phone to watch a video trailer for this book using that QR Code. The Cover QR code leads to book trailer http://bit.ly/2tfP1HN also found on Author website:

https://pattysadallah.com/other-books.

When the first edition was released, QR codes were relatively new technology, as was the concept of a book for which media was included. With technology being tricky for so many people, it grieves me to have learned how many people read my book without experiencing the film clips! Don't miss that blessing! So I knew I needed to make it easier for readers now.

All film clips can be found by going to my website https://PattySadallah.com/other-books and scroll to the Paperback Film Links tab. There you will find links categorized by page number, and clip title. So, keep your phone handy, and that page open and click the links as you arrive to them on the book pages.

All but one of the clips in this book are originals. The Christian Identity original "I Am" clip has been changed to "Identity" clip as the former was pulled from the internet by its creator. Still, the new clip in that category allowed me to share some important messages that were not included in the first version. Most of the new content will be identified as such.

The timing of this republication was catalyzed by *Clips That Move Mountains* winning the 2019 Enduring Light Gold Medal for Christian Insight in the Illumination Book Awards, sponsored by the Jenkins Group. I thank them for taking the time to review my book and for honoring me with this medal.

BACK STORY & INSTRUCTIONS

I had been writing a video blog for more than a year using short clips from mainstream Hollywood movies through <u>Wingclips.com</u>. The site has hundreds of short clips organized by movie title, theme and Bible verse. The 2- to 5-minute clips were fun, inspiring, thought-provoking, and made for easy writing.

On January 24, 2012, I got a call from a friend who had just read one of my blog articles. She mentioned that she liked my writing style and encouraged me to write a book. I had set out to write many books in my life, but always for the wrong reasons. I was a busy person so I thanked her, and I remember saying, "*If God wants me to write a book, He will make it abundantly clear.*"

Four hours later, God made it abundantly clear.

That night I was lying in bed and suddenly, I just got a flood of images, words, pictures and movies, rushing in my mind. I was lying awake just trying to process all of this for a few minutes and then I realized I needed to get up and journal it out. I wrote for about 2 hours.

The first thing that God gave me was the name of the book, **Clips that Move Mountains.** Then he gave me the map image with compass points North, West, South, and East and the words *"territory of impact."*

I knew it was supposed to be a book with videos being played inside of it. Seeing video and copy together is common on websites and even for my blog, but I had never seen that kind of book. I had no idea where to begin.

What is *Clips that Move Mountains*?

It was on Valentine's Day when God revealed to me that this book was really a love story. It was about the transformational nature of the love of Christ. Read on for the miracle of that story!

Every single believer has a calling and ministry right where they are. This is their territory of impact. The model that God gave me to write about shows how to expand your territory North, West, South, East, and most importantly, Center.

- Begin Center- Choose Jesus
- North- Growing your Faith in Christ
- West- Overcoming Life's Challenges and Finding Forgiveness
- South- Leveraging Life's Circumstances to Share your Faith and Light
- East- Using your Gifts to Help Others and Advance the Kingdom
- Back to Center- Living the Abundant Christian Life

Expanding your territory while you are here on earth will result in a life of abundance, Kingdom impact and multiplied blessings for eternity. God can't accomplish your purpose without your cooperation, and lots of Christians rob themselves of this abundant life and impact by not hearing or answering God's specific call for their lives.

There are inspirational stories from my life and others who have found their callings and have had miraculous impact. There are 23 clips in this book not counting the promotional videos in the Feature Filmmaker section in the back of the book. Many of them are from films that are based on true stories and are inspirational.

The life application sections will challenge you to go deeper with a journaling capacity so that you can write inside the book and save it as your own.

God's MUCH bigger vision

Being asked to write this book was a humbling and exciting calling! It is the strongest calling I've ever had in my life. When I started on the journey with this book, I thought that this was just me and God working together. I had been thinking much smaller than God on this one! But God made it clear that the video book project would be a ministry multiplier for Christian filmmakers, the cover artist, and other helping Christian organizations. So not only can you enjoy these clips, read about them and journal your own insights as part of the experience, but please visit the Featured Filmmaker and Other Artists section at the back of the book. There you can read about the talented ministries of these artists and filmmakers and view more clips and trailers about the films. I pray that you will be as inspired as I was by these films and that you will want to rent or buy them to share with others.

Why did God choose *me* to write this book? I have no idea. But I am grateful. Just like you, I am an ordinary person with specific gifts and passions. I have been an Organization Development Consultant for more than 30 years helping faith-based organizations move towards God's plans for them. Coaching people on finding their God-given callings has been a passion of mine for the last several years. The next Just Ask Jesus series book is *How to Find Your Calling.*

I may not know why God chose me to write this book, but I know that it is about falling in love and committing or recommitting your life to your One True Love, Jesus Christ. And it's about increasing your impact for Christ. Because the more we closely align our lives with the Lord, the more He will use us for His great purposes.

You may be reading this book because you just want to learn more about deepening your own relationship with God or because God has called you to disciple others in the faith. You may also have just gotten it because of the video clips, and you wanted to see what it was all about. God will meet you right where you are and move you closer to Him.

My purpose to write this book was ordained by God. My prayer is that you will find yours along the way by reading this book. I pray you will be blessed and transformed by Clips that Move Mountains. I hope that this book makes you think, laugh, cry, pray and serve the King with more effectiveness!

About the Movie Clips

God lives in the heart and not the head, so it's important to understand God through His language. When Jesus was on Earth He taught in stories and parables relative to the things that were important to people at the time. He still communicates that way. The language of the heart is pictures, stories, music and emotions. God is creative and desires to communicate to us in our present-day language. So, He will speak to us using words and pictures that are from our own culture, lives and time. This video book was entirely His idea! Why did He come up with this unique book concept? If a picture can be worth a thousand words, then a thought-provoking movie or video clip can be worth a million words. I guarantee you will remember the messages of the clips more than anything I have written about them.

Every clip is part of a film project that was created for its own purpose. God is interweaving those initial stand-alone projects with the purpose of this book project. If God would give me the inspiration to write about them, then I knew that they were on God's list!

God is using these movie clips to help instruct us all in the way to a closer relationship, forgiveness, opportunity and impact for the Kingdom. Seeds planted in our lifetime can bloom beyond our wildest imaginations for generations to come.

Clip Instructions

If you have a smart phone, tablet or computer, you can watch the videos by going to my website: www.PattySadallah.com and click on the **Other Books** tab and scroll down or click on the subtab **Paperback Film Clip Links** tab. All the clip links are there categorized by clip name and page number. Keep your phone or tablet handy while you read the book and you can watch the clips as you go. You must have internet access to watch the clips.

The URL's for each clip are in this book, so if you are reading the Kindle Version, you can simply click on the links as you read. Internet access is necessary to watch the films. So, keep that in mind when reading the book. If you choose to type these URL's into your search bar, type them carefully as they are case sensitive. Do not miss a blessing because you don't watch the clips. They really are the best!

Clip Disclaimer

The clips play from links connecting to a variety of different websites. Some are coming from the filmmakers' own websites, others from clip hosting services. I share this because if you have technical difficulties playing one of the clips, the problem is possibly with the streaming organization. They may be having trouble with their site or with this clip in general. My advice is to try it again a bit later. I do apologize in advance for technical frustration you may experience in viewing any of the clips.

Clips streaming from GodTube may require you to close out of your previous clip to make way for the next one. After clicking on your next clip, if you see the previous clip or an image of one you have already watched, simply click the "x" on the top right corner of the clip and your next clip will be ready to go.

If you have continued problems with a specific clip, please let me know by emailing Patty@PattySadallah.com. If a link is broken in the book, it is fixed on the website. Website links will work unless a clip creator decides to pull the clip from the web.

All scriptures in this book were found by using

www.BibleGateway.com. Scriptures and Jesus's voice in dialogue journaling examples are in *italics* for easy identification and unless otherwise indicated, they are from the New International Version (NIV).

LOVE, MIRACLES & IMPACT

God had given me the assignment to write the introduction section of this book, but I was confused. I had only been working on this book for a couple of weeks and personal experience told me that the introduction is something that you write last, not first. God was teaching me a lesson with this book about total surrender. I found that if I only did what God asked me to do, nothing more and nothing less, I could move forward. But, if I tried to do things my way or in my own timing, I would get stuck. God's process is different than mine and yours!

I was learning to go with God's flow. His ways are much wiser than ours, *1 Corinthians 1:25, "For the foolishness of God is wiser than human wisdom, and the weakness of God is stronger than human strength."* I was driving home after a church program and I knew that I had to finish the Introduction that day because it was my daily assignment from God. So, I prayed that God would tell me what He wanted me to write about and He brought to mind my salvation experience and a special letter.

The Beginning of my Love Story

When I was in college, I had a boyfriend named Fred, whom I worshiped. He was a Christian, and I wasn't yet. But he was

EVERYTHING to me. It was the tail end of freshman year and we had been together since the beginning of the year.

I was a member of a campus club that was participating in a planning retreat at a camp one weekend. Maureen was a couple years older than me and she was assigned as my roommate for the weekend. She was at this retreat representing a different campus group. We talked all night about God's love and his free gift of salvation. In the wee hours of the morning, I accepted Christ.

When I got back from that weekend, I was excited to share my decision with Fred. He had some news for me too. He told me that all weekend, he had gotten the sense that God wanted him to break up with me. He didn't know why but felt strongly that he needed to do it. I was devastated.

I immediately called Maureen and she told me that she was expecting my call. God had told her that Fred was going to break up with me and she had a letter for me. It was a letter from God about how He needed to be my first love. It was exactly what I needed. Maureen worked and prayed with me for several months teaching me from the Bible and helping me learn more about God.

Just when I was feeling better, I called Maureen on the same number that I had been calling her for months and a strange guy answered the phone. He said that they didn't know who Maureen was and that they had that number all year. I was confused. I searched for her contact information in the school registration office and could find no record of her. It seemed like she didn't exist. Had God used an angel to lead me to Him? I have always thought so. *Hebrews 13:2* says *"Don't forget to show hospitality to strangers, for some who have done this have entertained angels without realizing it!"* I never saw her again, but I look forward to seeing her in heaven some day and then I will know for sure.

I had that dog-eared letter for years, and gave copies of it away to many people who had broken hearts and needed to know that God loved them. A part of me thought that Fred and I would get back together when we were both spiritually ready. But that wasn't God's plan.

George and I married 7 years later. As soon as I moved into our newlywed home, I lost that letter. It had been in my Bible all that time, and then suddenly, it was gone. I was heartbroken. It had become one of my treasured possessions. I had guessed that I lost it because God felt like I didn't need it anymore. But I have thought of it often. It had been lost to me for 25 years.

So, I'm back in the car asking God what He wants me to write for the introduction and He brings to mind this letter. I remember asking Him out loud, "God, are you planning on putting that letter in my hands again after all of these years?" I was filled with glory bumps of anticipation. I had looked for it on the Internet over the years a few times and I was never able to find it.

I prayed that God would let me see that letter again and if He did, I would absolutely include it in the book. So, I came home and typed into the Google search bar the only words that I remember from that letter "I am God. Believe it and be satisfied." THERE IT WAS, right in front of me, the exact letter that I had 32 years ago. *"Take delight in the Lord, and He will give you the desires of your heart." – Psalm 37:4*

I have no idea who posted it on the Internet originally. The Internet reference amuses me because it said the letter was "originally posted on an online blog." God had given it to me in 1979, long before the Internet was even conceived.

Here is that love letter...

> *Everyone longs to give themselves completely to someone — to have a deep soul relationship with another, to be loved thoroughly and exclusively. But God, to a Christian says:*
>
> *"No, not until you are satisfied and fulfilled and content with being loved by Me alone. I love you, my child, and until you discover that only in Me is your satisfaction to be found, you will not be capable of the perfect human relationship that I have planned for you. You will never be united with another until you are united with Me — exclusive of anyone or anything else, exclusive of any other desires or longings. I want you to stop planning, stop wishing, and allow Me to give you the most thrilling plan existing — one that you can't imagine. I want you to have the best. Please allow Me to bring it to you. Just keep experiencing that satisfaction knowing that I AM. Keep learning and listening to the things I tell you . . . You must wait.*
>
> *Don't be anxious. Don't worry. Don't look around at the things others have gotten or that I've given to them. Don't look at the things you think you want. You just keep looking off and away up to Me, or you'll miss what I want to show you.*

And then, when you're ready, I'll surprise you with a love far more wonderful than any would ever dream. You see, until you are ready and until the one I have for you is ready, I am working even this very minute to have both of you ready at the same time. Until you are both satisfied exclusively with Me and with the life I have prepared for you, you won't be able to experience the love that exemplifies your relationship with Me...and this is perfect love.

And dear one, I want you to have this most wonderful love, I want you to see in flesh a picture of your relationship with Me, and to enjoy materially and concretely the everlasting union of beauty and perfection and love that I offer you with Myself.

Know that I love you utterly, I am God. Believe it and be satisfied."

I hope that it speaks to your heart like it did mine more than 30 years ago! This was the beginning of many miracles that God showed me through the process of writing this book.

Whether Maureen was an angel or not, she certainly was the messenger that gave this precious letter from God to me.

This Maureen story begged an update. Once I learned how to have direct Jesus encounters in the Special Place*, the Lord used those experiences to heal me of some heart wounds. Here is an experience that I had with the Lord that not only proved to me that Maureen was my angel, but that healed that past hurt.

I was working on a deliverance class called "Prayers the Heal the Heart" for my doctorate. I had some work to do to heal some heart wounds. I met Jesus in my Special Place in the Spirit. He and I walked up the hill to the Sea of Galilee. Then, we laid on the ground and were looking and laughing at the clouds. Jesus thought that one looked like an elephant and I thought it looked like a duck. I was thinking about the people in the book (referencing the class book) that shared that God had healed them of past memories by going back to the scene and allowing Him to reframe the circumstance and show them truth they didn't see before.

You can ask Me to show you anything that you want to know.

Lord, as painful as it is, to take me back to my heartbreak in 1979. Please show me where you were then as Maureen and I were talking and when you gave me the love letter.

Immediately, I was back in 1979, watching the scene play out the way I knew it, there but not really there.

I saw myself crying face down on my bed in my dorm room. I looked around and could see with great detail remembering what the room looked like. Then I saw Jesus lying next to me as I sobbed, and He was whispering in my ear. I walked over closer so I could hear what He was saying to me. He was speaking word for word the letter that I received in 1979. At that same moment I saw the words being typed in the upper right corner of my mind's eye. As Jesus spoke the words, they were appearing on the paper in heaven. Then I saw Jesus giving the paper to Maureen.

Then the Lord gave me short vignette glimpses of Maureen and I as she gave me the letter, and of us studying the Word together.

Then I saw myself trying to call her and Jesus was standing

next to me when I was talking to the guy who answered the phone. I was confused as he said he had that number all school year. As I heard myself talking to the man on the phone, Jesus was whispering in my ear... *"You don't need her anymore... you have Me now..."* He was repeating that in my ear as I hung up the phone in lost confusion.

Wow, Lord. That really helps me understand this situation so much more. You were with me the entire time! Please show me Maureen now so I can thank her for what she did for me.

Suddenly, we were back at the Secret place still lying on the grass and we sat up on the hill and He pointed toward the Sea and I saw Maureen walking up the hill to greet us. She was dressed in Roman dress with a breastplate of armor and had long dark and flowing hair. She looked a bit like I remember her, but didn't have glasses, and she still looked young. She hugged me and I hugged her and could feel her wings... soft, strong and powerful. She had a meekness about her, strength under control.

Then the Lord gave me short images of Maureen with me as a child sitting on my bed as I was crying because I could hear my parents fighting, and another where she was sitting and laughing as my sibs and I were hanging our feet off the back of our powder blue station wagon. And I saw her with Jesus when He gave her the letter and the assignment to share it with me.

Just like Me, she has been with you all along. She is your Guardian Angel.

I thanked them both and cried... it was an overwhelming vision! THANKS LORD! Maureen and I have had many adventures together since then. Not the least of which was experiencing what the shepherds saw on the night of Jesus' birth. Ask, seek and knock and you can have Jesus adventures like this, too!

(*For a guided imagery experience where I take you to discovering your Special Place of encountering Jesus go to:

https://pattysadallah.com/just-ask-jesus/ and click on the media link entitled "Special Place" or if reading the Kindle version, click here:

https://app.box.com/file/215030946100

I have written much more about how to have intimate conversations and encounters with Jesus in the How to Live a Worry-Free Life: Just ask Jesus Series Book 1.

If you are interested in learning more about angels, I recommend a great book called Everyday Angels by Dr. Charity Virkler Kayembe and Joe Brock. This book shares the Biblical truth of how angels intercede and help us on a day-to-day basis.

This book is all about God's love story with you and me. In fact, the whole point of God creating people in the first place was His love. He created the heavens and the earth and everything in it just so He could create people to have a relationship. He gave us free will so that we could choose to love Him back. God desired an intimate relationship with His people so much that He sent His son Jesus to redeem us so that we could spend eternity with Him in heaven. My prayer is that you will fall in love or deepen your love for God in the process of experiencing this book.

Miracles are Signs of God's Love and Power

As remarkable as it is that God decided to bring Jolene back from the dead after 1 hour; that is not the biggest miracle of this family story. Anthony had accepted Christ 15 years before the accident but had allowed his faith to go dormant. So much so that the people closest to him didn't even know that he was saved. He had let his faith be hidden, even to himself.[1]

Jolene had been dead for 45 minutes after a horrible car crash and the doctors and trauma nurses were exhausted from trying to get her back. They tried to convince Anthony that she was gone and that reviving her now would leave her vegetative. He could not accept that his fiancé was dead. Anthony dropped to his knees, raised his arms and prayed out loud nonstop for about 15 minutes. His children were confused; they had never seen dad pray like that before.

After being dead for a little more than an hour, the machines monitoring Jolene's vitals sprang to life. Jolene was back. After some time in a coma and a few months of paralysis, Jolene slowly but surely regained her functioning. Jolene awoke to a new Anthony; one who was on fire for God, much different than the man she had known. It didn't take long for Jolene to accept Christ as her Lord and Savior, and she has been transformed, too. God had saved Jolene physically, and then spiritually.

Everyone was shocked and surprised at the change in Anthony. He had been transformed by the love and grace of Jesus Christ. People surrounding Anthony began to accept Christ too: his two daughters, their babysitter, and Jolene's best friend. Anthony's transformation and impact for Christ was the bigger miracle.

Miracles, signs and wonders are all over the Bible. *Psalm*

77:14 says, "You are the God who performs miracles; you display your power among the peoples." But, is God still performing miracles today like the one that Anthony prayed for? Absolutely, much more that you may realize! The power to do miracles comes from the Holy Spirit and when the will of God and the faith to pray bold prayers line up, God shows up in mighty ways. God uses miracles to display His glory, power and might, all for His good purposes.

Jesus instructs us about the power to do miracles in *Matthew 21:19-22*, when He curses a fig tree,

"18 Early in the morning, as Jesus was on His way back to the city, He was hungry. 19 Seeing a fig tree by the road, He (Jesus) went up to it but found nothing on it except leaves. Then He said to it, 'May you never bear fruit again!' Immediately the tree withered. 20 When the disciples saw this, they were amazed. 'How did the fig tree wither so quickly?' they asked. 21 Jesus replied, "Truly I tell you, if you have faith and do not doubt, not only can you do what was done to the fig tree, but also you can say to this mountain, 'Go, throw yourself into the sea,' and it will be done. 22 If you believe, you will receive whatever you ask for in prayer."

And when Jesus healed the demon-possessed boy in *Matthew 17:19-20*, *"Then afterward the disciples asked Jesus privately, "Why couldn't we cast out that demon?"[20] "You don't have enough faith," Jesus told them. "I tell you the truth, if you had faith even as small as a mustard seed, you could say to this mountain, 'Move from here to there,' and it would move. Nothing would be impossible."*

I pray that you will have the faith to move mountains as you progress on your journey to a greater understanding of the power and promises of God. This power is accessible to EVERY believer. Yes, even you!

Pray for Rain- Clip from Faith like Potatoes

Angus Buchan is no stranger to miracles. Miracles have surrounded him since his spiritual rebirth in 1979. He was a hotheaded white South African during a time when racial tensions were heightened by a struggling farming economy due to a drought. Faced with ever mounting challenges, hardships and personal turmoil, Angus quickly spiraled down into a life consumed by anger, fear and destruction.

It was not until he heard the honest witnessing of a man who seemed just like him who had found peace and joy in Jesus Christ that Angus gave his life to Christ. Immediately, he had an unquenchable hunger and thirst to know God and spent many hours reading The Word and praying. Learning about this Jesus, His Savior, Redeemer and Friend was a consuming passion.

Angus believed God. He didn't just believe IN God. He believed God. For every promise he read about in the Bible, Angus trusted God to be who He said He was.

"I had a choice: I could believe the lies of the devil, in which case I was on my way to suicide, or I could believe in the promises of God, and be taken through my time of trial." ~ Angus Buchan, *Faith like Potatoes: The Story of a Farmer Who Risked Everything for God.*

One of the first miracles Angus experienced as a new believer in Christ is depicted in this clip from *Faith like Potatoes* about the true story of his life. Angus prayed for rain during a severe drought to stop a fire that threatened to take his farm.

Pray for Rain

http://bit.ly/2GzdXC2 [2]

See PattySadallah.com Other Books tab Paperback Film Links, Pray for Rain

Angus began quoting the Scripture promise found in Matthew and Mark *out loud* to God. *Matthew 21:22, "If you believe, you will receive whatever you ask for in prayer,"* and reinforced again in *Mark 11:24, "Therefore I tell you, whatever you ask for in prayer, believe that you have received it, and it will be yours."*

Then Angus began to pray for rain.

There is power in prayer. When men work, they work. But when men pray, God works." ~ Angus Buchan.

Potatoes need a lot of water to grow. It doesn't make sense to plant them in the dust of a drought dried land. People thought that Angus was crazy for wanting to plant them. When he was questioned about this decision Angus answered, "The condition for a miracle is difficulty, however the condition for a great miracle is not difficulty, but impossibility." He believed God for this miracle and God loves to answer bold faithful prayers.

Potatoes are a wonderful metaphor for faith because they

grow underground. When you can't see the progress toward your goal or when the progress is hidden from your view, you still have to trust God. Angus planted those potatoes in the dust, and it didn't rain during that drought season. There was no reason to believe that potatoes would grow in that 4-month drought. But on harvest day, there was a bumper crop of potatoes the size of double fists! God is glorified when we believe Him for great miracles. He delights in showing up to answer bold prayers!

Angus Buchan can't stop sharing about the saving grace of Jesus Christ and the ripple effect is rocking heaven! He is a powerfully effective Evangelist in Africa. In 1980, Angus and his wife Jill started Shalom Ministries. The main purpose of the ministry is to go out and preach in South Africa and Africa. It began with only 40 people and grew exponentially. By the sixth conference more than 200,000 gathered and by its seventh and final conference the following year (2010), it seated more than 400,000. Since the completion of the conferences, other believers have been inspired to hold similar events.[3]

For some, like me, spiritual growth is slow and gradual. God grabs you by the heart and you change one day at a time. Others are more like Jamie Grace, who in 2012 at age 20 is the youngest Grammy nominated Christian Contemporary artist. She accepted God's gift of grace as a small child and ran boldly with it at a young age. Her music and delightful personality are contagious. I don't know why, but most days her songs are stuck in my head!

And others are more like Anthony. They accept Christ, but at least for a while, don't let God truly change them. Then God gets their attention abruptly and they are never the same. Unfortunately, many people who have accepted Christ's salvation can live their entire lives keeping their gift a secret and are robbed of the fullness in Christ that is theirs by way of inheritance as a child of the Living God.

It took me 30 years to be bold enough to lead a ministry and another 2 years for God to give me the assignment to write this book. It took a life changing crisis for God to change Anthony Lakota from a man who kept his faith hidden to a man who is on fire for sharing the Good News of God's amazing grace. Angus was a man at the end of himself who saw the hope in another man's victory. However God gets your attention, the common denominator is a consuming passion to share the truth and promises of the Living God.

God still does miraculous things through and because of faithful ordinary people who believe Him for His promises. In fact, every believer in Christ, even you and me, can be surrounded by miracles too. All we have to do is believe God for His promises.

This book is a love story; yours with Jesus and mine with Jesus. Are you wondering when your love story begins? Keep reading and watching the clips in this book. It is my prayer that you will meet and fall in love with Jesus too and be ready to pray the salvation prayer found in the Center chapter of this book.

Ordinary People/Extraordinary Impact

What do Angus Buchan, the Apostles, and you and I all have in common? We are all ordinary people. Even though the Apostles were able to do miracles as great as Jesus did when He was on the earth, that didn't make them super human because it wasn't them actually performing those signs and wonders. *Acts 19:11, "God gave Paul the power to perform unusual miracles." And He-*

brews 2:4 "And God confirmed the message by giving signs and wonders and various miracles and gifts of the Holy Spirit whenever He chose." The power comes from the Holy Spirit; the very same Holy Spirit that lives in the hearts of each and every believer of Jesus Christ.

You don't have to perform a miracle to do something that you simply would never be able to do by your own strength. God's plans for you are big. They are much bigger thaN you and I would ever shoot for on our own. In our own flesh, we would never be able to accomplish them. But in God's power, as *Philippians 4:13* reminds us, *"We can do all things through Christ who gives us strength."*

God has a plan for you. His Word promises it. *Jeremiah 29:11, "For I know the plans I have for you,' declares the Lord, "plans to prosper you and not to harm you, plans to give you hope and a future."* God has one big plan that intertwines all of us. The next video clip will show you how.

God's One Big Plan: Strangers clip

We may not think about it often, but our lives intertwine with others without our even being aware. *Strangers* is a short film that demonstrates that reality.

Strangers

http://bit.ly/1crPDNp [4]

See PattySadallah.com Other Books tab, Paperback Film Links, Strangers

How cool is it that our stories intertwine like that without us even having an idea that there is a connection? One day in heaven I believe that God will show all believers these connections and we will be amazed at the unseen impact that our faithful interventions have had on others.

People need Jesus for all kinds of reasons. Some need to find Him so that they can find forgiveness and let go of horrendous injustices in their past. Others have been the perpetrators of horrible hurts on others and desperately need to forgive themselves and change into better people. Some just feel lost and need God's direction; they know that there is a purpose for their lives and just feel like nomads wandering hopelessly. Others respond to the well-lived life of a Christian influencer and just want to have what that person has to live a life of abundant joy and satisfaction.

The point is that ALL of us need God's love. There isn't a person on this planet that hasn't sinned save for Jesus Christ.

Each of us needs the love of God and every one of us can and will become a better person with the power of the Holy Spirit if we let Him in and let Him do a good work in us.

I love that this clip not only showed a variety of people who needed Christ for very different reasons, but it also showed that the method for reaching people is as different as the people themselves. Some people respond to one-on-one conversations with transformed believers who can speak the truth in love. Some accept the gift of salvation because they heard someone's life-changing testimony at a church service on TV or the Internet. Some are drawn by the Holy Spirit while reading the pages of the Bible or another Christian book. And still others are brought to their knees in a moment of desperation and reach to God for help.

It's important to note that it is the Holy Spirit who completes the transaction. It is not you or me. We don't want to take the credit for someone's salvation decision. We all play our part in the process in our own ways. Some help to prepare hearts for accepting the gift of salvation by answering questions about Jesus or the Bible. Others have the privilege of leading someone into the kingdom, as so many did in this clip. All roles played along the way are as important as all others. Every one of us is gifted in different ways and God uses every believer uniquely to help people find their way to Jesus. The East chapter will cover lots of ways that you can use your gifts to honor God and have eternal impact.

Being a Godly example is a critical way that we can help direct people to the Father. Christians who live hypocritical lives do major damage to the cause of leading people to Christ. While no one is perfect this side of heaven, if you are a publicly professed Christian, your behavior may be the only Bible that people ever read. So be aware that people are watching you. *Romans 14:21 New King James Version (NKJV), "It is good neither to eat meat nor drink wine nor do anything by which your brother stumbles or is offended or is made weak."*

Our impact is not limited to our own lifetimes. Little prayer warrior grannies from centuries ago are still reaping their multiplying impact. Until the day that Christ returns and it's time for us to have our final judgment with the Heavenly Father, our impact is still being racked up. I think the Apostle Paul will be quite surprised on that day when he sees how many people are in the kingdom because of his faithfulness. He could have never predicted that his letters to those small home churches on three continents would become the majority of the New Testament. Or that the Bible would eventually be translated into every tongue and shared in every nation for untold generations so that multitudes would be able to learn how to have a relationship with a Holy God.

We are all connected by God's one big plan. God's plan includes all of us. He can do His will without you, but you miss an unimaginable list of blessings if you don't participate with His perfect will for you. *Luke 11:33, "No one lights a lamp and puts it in a place where it will be hidden, or under a bowl. Instead they put it on its stand, so that those who come in may see the light."* If God has blessed you, share it with people and see what God will do with your faithfulness!

Your Promised Land & The Territory of Christian Impact Model

Some years ago, I attended a Beth Moore Bible study entitled

"The Inheritance."[5] As always, I learned a lot from Beth's relatable style and in- depth Biblical analysis. The point of the entire program was that when you accept Jesus Christ as your Lord and Savior, you become a child of the living God. All children of the living God are entitled to a great inheritance. The term "promised land" is used more than 300 times in the Bible referencing promises of this great inheritance. I can't do justice to her study in these few paragraphs, but they are important background to the Territory of Christian Impact Model and why it's relevant to this video book.

One of the things that I learned in Beth's class is that the "promised land" included three things: God's Presence, Property and People.[6] In the days of the Old Testament, the focus of the inheritance was external riches.

- **The Presence of God:** *Joshua 1:9, "Have I not commanded you? Be strong and courageous. Do not be terrified; do not be discouraged, for the Lord your God will be with you wherever you go."*

- **Property**: In the Old Testament days, property was physical land the Israelites were promised after God rescued them from Egypt. And after Jesus' resurrection, the focus of "promised land" shifts to more internal riches. Since the Holy Spirit dwells within each believer, we now have power to live the abundant Christian life of victory. This is described as the "Fruit of the Spirit." *Galatians 5:22-23, "But the fruit of the Spirit is love, joy, peace, patience, kindness, goodness, faithfulness, gentleness and self-control. Against such things there is no law."* In all cases, satisfaction comes with productivity. Land can't bear fruit without hard work and people can't bear fruit without hard work. So, this side of the cross, our promised land is our Christian impact.

- **People:** *Genesis 2:18, "The Lord God said, "'It is not good that man should be alone; I will make Him a helper comparable to Him."* God wants us to live in families and communities. He wants us to work side by side with others and He knits together all of us in one big plan. God has a team in mind to help us accomplish His plan for us.

If we want to reach our promised land today, we must live out the big plan that God has promised for each of us with the power of the Holy Spirit. Our heavenly inheritance is based on it. What happens here on earth will affect your final resting place in heaven. If you accept Jesus Christ as your Lord and Savior, you will live in heaven forever. We are saved by faith and not by works. But, if you live a life purposed to serve God and do His will, then you will have much better accommodations when in heaven. If you accept Christ and live your own way, don't follow His perfect plan for you and keep your Savior a best kept secret, your heavenly house will still be nicer than anything you can imagine. But, it will be less than the more faithful people's eternal residences. Jesus instructed about this in the parable of the three servants.

Matthew 25:14-30 New Living Translation (NLT)

Parable of the Three Servants

$_{14}$*"Again, the Kingdom of Heaven can be illustrated by the story of a man going on a long trip. He called together his servants and entrusted his money* to them while he was gone. [15] He gave five bags of silver[a] to one, two bags of silver to another and one bag of silver to the last—dividing it in proportion to their abilities. He then left on his trip.

[16] "The servant who received the five bags of silver began to invest the money and earned five more. [17] The servant with two bags of silver also went to work and earned two more. [18] But the servant who received the one bag of silver dug a hole in the ground and hid the master's money.

[19] "After a long time their master returned from his trip and called them to give an account of how they had used his money. [20] The servant to whom he had entrusted the five bags of silver came forward with five more and said, 'Master, you gave me five bags of silver to invest, and I have earned five more.'

[21] "The master was full of praise. 'Well done, my good and faithful servant. You have been faithful in handling this small amount, so now I will give you many more responsibilities. Let's celebrate together! [b]'

[22] "The servant who had received the two bags of silver came forward and said, 'Master, you gave me two bags of silver to invest, and I have earned two more.'

[23] "The master said, 'Well done, my good and faithful servant. You have been faithful in handling this small amount, so now I will give you many more responsibilities. Let's celebrate together!

$_{24}$ "Then the servant with the one bag of silver came and said, 'Master, I knew you were a harsh man, harvesting crops you didn't plant and gathering crops you didn't cultivate. $_{25}$ I was afraid I would lose your money, so I hid it in the earth. Look, here is your money back.'"

$_{26}$ "But the master replied, 'You wicked and lazy servant! If you knew I harvested crops I didn't plant and gathered crops I didn't cultivate, $_{27}$ why didn't you deposit my money in the bank? At least I could have gotten some interest on it.'

$_{28}$ "Then he ordered, 'Take the money from this servant, and give it to the one with the ten bags of silver. $_{29}$ To those who use well what they are given, even more will be given, and they will have abundance. But from those who do nothing, even what little they have will be taken away. $_{30}$ Now throw this useless servant into outer darkness, where there will be weeping and gnashing of teeth.'

We have established that our promised land is living out the plans God has for us and our heavenly inheritance is connected to whether we do that or not. We have established that we have God's presence and people to help us. That goes a long way to saying *what* leads to an abundant Christian life. The question on the table now is *how* do we get there?

When I was journaling the download from God about writing this book, He popped this compass model back into my mind. I had learned something similar from Beth Moore in the Inheritance class. At first I only saw the North, West, South and East of the model. The compass was a metaphor for the

Promised Land. I remember seeing it and asking out loud, "But, isn't this Beth's model?" God reminded me that He gave it to Beth in the first place. It would take a month for God to give me the Center part of the model and reveal that this book is a love story. It took more than a year for the puzzle pieces to come together and make the details clear of what He actually wanted me to write about.

God gave me the Territory of Christian Impact Model as an adaptation of Beth Moore's diagram in her Inheritance Bible study as a roadmap for you in this video book. It answers the question: HOW do you live the life that God has planned for you?

The Territory of Christian Impact Model

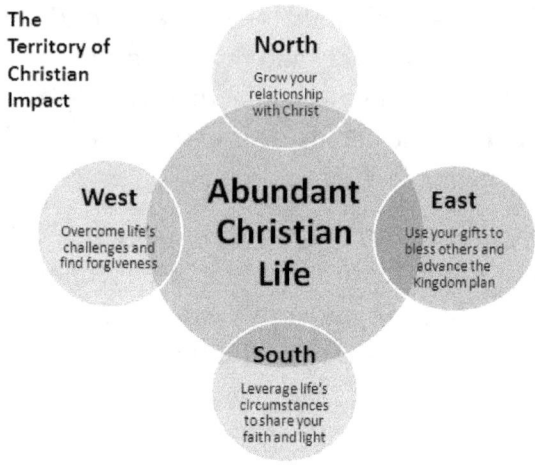

Each of the next five chapters will address a component of this model. We will begin at the center and then work counterclockwise around the model and wind back up in the Center again. This entire model represents your land. To the degree that you can stretch yourself:

- **Begin Center** by choosing Jesus and accepting God's free gift of Salvation,

- **North** by growing your relationship with Christ,

- **West** by overcoming life's challenges and finding forgiveness,

- **South** by leveraging life's circumstances to share your light and faith,

- **East** by using your gifts to bless others and advance the Kingdom, you will push the land boundary of your abundant Christian life to it's full potential. This will lead to a more productive and fulfilling life now and a much bigger eternal reward in heaven, and returning...
- **Back to Center** where as you grow in all of the other areas, your impact grows both here on earth and in heaven.

As I said before, this book is a love story; yours with Jesus and mine with Jesus. The moment that God grabs your heart is the beginning of your love story, and what you do and how you allow it to change your life is your love story. It is also a roadmap for how to increase your territory of impact for Christ. When you grow North, West, South and East, your Center will grow too. You will experience the abundant Christian life in greater proportion and your land of promise will increase on earth as it is in heaven.

The model will guide us on our journey to increase our territory of impact for Christ. We will first look at what it takes to fall in love with Jesus and how to surrender your life to Him. Then, we will look at all it takes to truly grow your relationship in Christ. We will move on to how to overcome the challenges of life with the help and strength of the Almighty God. We will learn how to be the moon and reflect God's grace and light in everyday circumstances. And finally, we will learn how to use our God-given gifts to accomplish God's purposes in our lives.

Discipleship

This book is about impact for Christ. None of us will truly know what our impact was in this world until Judgment Day. Think about it. The Apostle Paul encountered Jesus on the road to Damascus and it changed his life.

Paul spent the rest of his life making sure that as many people as he encountered would know that Jesus was the Messiah, the Only Way. Jesus changed Paul's life and He could change your life too if you accepted his free gift of grace. Paul traveled, preached and wrote letters to "churches" and people that he encountered. God revealed a lot of Himself to Paul.

But God never told Paul, 'by the way, in hundreds of years, I'm going to make sure that a bunch of Christians pull together some key God-breathed messages that I have given to you and a handful of prophets, and they are going to make them into the New Testament and this will be joined with the Torah. I'm going to have them call it the Holy Bible and it will be one story from beginning to end, more consistent than any other written work. It will be translated into every language and spread to every nation in the world so the millions and millions of people will hear the Good News of the Gospel and be saved. Your ministry, Paul, will reach thousands of years past your death.' I hope I get to see Paul's face when he learns that reality on Judgment Day!

Your impact is NOT limited by your own lifespan.

If you are a Christian, you have your own story about how God met you and changed your heart. Did He change your life? The degree to which you answer that question is the work of this book. Keep reading and watching the clips in this book and it is my prayer that you will meet and fall in love with Jesus too and be ready to pray the salvation prayer found at the end of this book.

Salvation is a free gift, but it is not cheap. Nothing has ever been more costly. We are robbing ourselves and countless others if we don't make the very most out of this life to advance the Kingdom.

This book is about falling in love and committing or recommitting your life to your one True Love and it's about increasing your impact for Christ. It is a "how-to" book for growing that special relationship with God and how to become more like Christ each day so He can change you into the person you were created to be. The more we closely align our lives with the Lord, the more He will use us for His great purposes.

You may be reading this book because you just want to learn more about deepening your own relationship with God. Or, you may be reading because God has called you to disciple others in the faith and this book can be used for you to help others. God will meet you right where you are and move you closer to Him.

This is a journey, and I am happy that you have decided to come along side me because this book is also about legacy and God's craftmanship of weaving individuals and passions and projects into one beautiful story.

I hope you will take the time to do the Life Application Study homework at the end of each section. You can write your answers to the study questions right into your book and resave it as your personal discipleship journal. You will be blessed to see what God has for you as you dive deeper into the Living Word.

Let's get going!

Life Application: LOVE, MIRACLES & IMPACT

1. Think about your first love. Describe how you felt being in love. Reflect on how you spent your time, what you treasured about that person and what made you happy in that relationship.

2. Share what you learned about God from the love letter that He gave to us.

3. Share about a miracle you've been close to — either in your own life or someone else. What were the circumstances that made you consider it a miracle? Reflect on how God was at work in that situation. What do you think it took for Angus Buchan and Anthony Lakota to believe God for their miracles?

4. What did you take away from the *Strangers* clip? Can you see yourself in any of those characters? Can you think back on a time when God was using you in a small way that made a difference in someone's life without you being aware of it at the time? Share a time when someone was reaching out to you.

BEGIN CENTER
Choose Jesus

What is the abundant Christian life and why should we want it? Let's see how the Bible describes it. We will look at the same verse in two different Bible translations so you can see what God intends the life of the Christian to look like.

The first version is *Galatians 5:22-23* from the Amplified Bible. The Amplified Bible adds explanation phrases to help people understand the meaning of the verse.

> *Galatians 5:22 (AMP) "But the fruit of the [Holy] Spirit [the work which His presence within accomplishes] is love, joy (gladness), peace, patience (an even temper, forbearance), kindness, goodness, (benevolence), faithfulness, $_{23}$ Gentleness (meekness, humility), self-control. (self-restraint, continence). Against such things there is no law [[a]that can bring a charge]."*

Next is the same section of Scripture from The Message. The Message is a Bible version that is written in today's vernacular. This also aids in understanding.

> *Galatians 5:22-23 (MSG) $_{22-23}$ "But what happens*

> when we live God's way? He brings gifts into our lives, much the same way that fruit appears in an orchard — things like affection for others, exuberance about life, serenity. We develop willingness to stick with things, a sense of compassion in the heart, and a conviction that a basic holiness permeates things and people. We find ourselves involved in loyal commitments, not needing to force our way in life, able to marshal and direct our energies wisely."

In order to have the abundant Christian life, you must first admit that you need God. You must then accept the gift of salvation. When you do, the Holy Spirit will be permanently deposited in your heart. His presence will never leave you or forsake you. *Deuteronomy 31:6, "Be strong and courageous. Do not be afraid or terrified because of them, for the Lord your God goes with you; He will **never leave** you nor **forsake** you,"* (bold emphasis mine). This exact phrase is mentioned at least five other times in the NIV and the concept is in the Bible 84 times. Think of it like a tether ball. No matter how hard you try to throw that ball away, it's still tethered to the pole. No matter how hard a Christian tries to push God away, He is ALWAYS still there.

When the Holy Spirit takes up residence in your heart, He begins to mold you into the characteristics mentioned above. This is called the Fruit of the Spirit. Notice that it's not called the Fruits of the Spirit. A tree bears one type of fruit, not a lot of different types of fruit. God has *one* character so it is called the Fruit of the Spirit.

As we become more Christ-like we begin to change in each

of those areas. Could you benefit from more patience? Do you love others or yourself as much as you could? How about "that thing" that you continually struggle with in your life; would a bit of self-control allow you to have more victory in that area? I don't know about you, but I've never met a person who couldn't benefit from being more like the characteristics of the Fruit of the Spirit. The Fruit of the Spirit is God's character.

This list shows us the heart of God. We will never be perfect this side of heaven, but we can be slowly but surely transformed into this character if we allow the Holy Spirit to do His good work in us.

It is true that He is always ready to help you when you call on Him. Still, you must include Him; ask and allow the Holy Spirit to guide you and direct you along the path that God has created uniquely for you to be transformed by Him. You will become more like God along the way when you surrender more and more of yourself to Him. I like to think of it as onion layers. There will always be a layer that can be peeled off to make us a better and better version of our best selves.

In this chapter, we will address the head and the heart of the matter of choosing Jesus, and we will look at the transformational nature of God. The goal is to enlarge your inner circle on the Territory of Christian Impact by expanding to the North, West, South and East circles. In doing so, you will increase your Fruit of the Spirit, and be able to find the satisfaction and the victory in life that God intended for you.

I don't know where you are in the process, but let's compare it to a temperature scale. If you are an atheist, and don't believe in God at all, you would be on the cold end of the spectrum. If you are Christian but tend to hide your faith from others and don't really include God much in your life, you may be lukewarm on the spectrum. If you are on fire to serve God and love the Lord with all your heart, you would be on the hot scale. Wherever you are right now, your goal should be to move toward the hotter end of the spectrum because that's where the blessings of the abundant life reside.

Why Choose Jesus? Prophetic Proof Clip

Is it logical to choose Jesus? People who maintain that Christianity is for people who need a crutch or think that believing in Jesus is illogical have simply not done their homework. Just as you and I have a fingerprint that is unique to each of us, Jesus is the only person who could have fulfilled all prophesies written more than 700 years before his birth. Check out just some of the Old Testaments Prophesies that foretold Jesus as the one true Messiah in this *Prophetic Proof* clip from Echoing Praise Ministries.

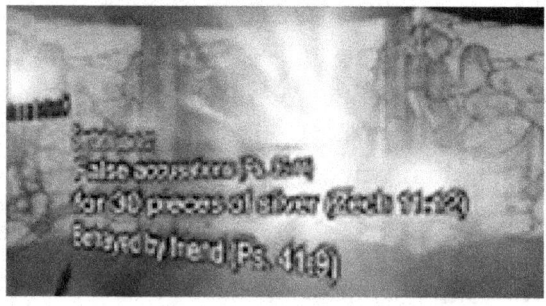

http://bit.ly/1fXiVpw [7]

PattySadallah.com Other Books tab Paperback Film Links, Prophetic Proof

Wow, that is pretty amazing, isn't it? Let's dig into it a bit. Eighteenth Century English Theologian and Oxford Professor, Henry Parry Liddon, did the research and found 332 prophesies that Jesus fulfilled.[8] Of these, 29 were fulfilled in the last 24 hours of His life. What was Liddon's conclusion? *"It is only Jesus Christ who has thrown light on life and immortality through the gospel; and because He has done so and has enabled us by His atoning death and intercession to make the most of this discovery, His gospel is, for all who will, a power of God unto salvation."* ~Henry Parry Liddon

I'm not sure if Professor of Mathematics, Peter Stoner was inspired by the work of Henry Liddon or not, but in 1969, he wrote a book called *Science Speaks*.[9] In his book, Dr. Stoner calculated the probability that any one man could fulfill just eight messianic prophecies to be one chance in 10 to the 17th power, meaning a one with 17 zeros after it.

Dr. Stoner gave this illustration to help people understand what that mathematical likelihood would be: cover the entire state of Texas (268,820 square miles) with silver dollars up to two feet deep. The total number of silver dollars needed would be 10 to the 17th power. Next, mark one silver dollar so it can be easily identified and put it back. Then thoroughly stir all the silver dollars all over the state. Finally, blindfold someone and tell them they can travel anywhere that they want in Texas, but they must pick up only one of the silver dollars. The chance of finding that one marked silver dollar in a 2-foot deep pile covering the entire state of Texas would be the same statistical chance the prophets had for just eight prophecies coming true in any one man in the future. I don't know about you, but I would have trouble finding a marked silver dollar in a 2-ft by 2-ft box with my eyes open!

Dr. Stoner submitted his figures for review to a Committee at the American Scientific Affiliation. After examining his figures, they verified that his calculations were dependable and accurate for the scientific material presented. And that is just eight of the 332 prophecies about the Messiah that Jesus fulfills!

What were some of those prophesies? The first listed verse in each bullet was the Old Testament prophesy, and the second verse is the New Testament fulfillment. Let's look at just some of the prophecies that happened in the last 24 hours of Jesus' life:[11]

- *Sold for 30 pieces of silver (Zechariah 11:12; Matt. 26:14-15)*

- *The money to be cast to the potter (Zechariah 11:13; Matt. 27:3-10)*

- *The disciples to forsake Him (Zechariah 13:7; Matt. 26:56, Mark 14:27)*

- *He was silent before His accusers (Isaiah 53:7; Matt. 27:12-14)*

- *He was wounded and bruised (Isaiah 53:5; Matt. 27:12-14)*

- *His hands and feet to be pierced (Psalm 22:16; Luke 23:33; John 20:25-27)*

- *He was crucified with thieves (Isaiah 53:12; Mark 15:27-28)*

- *He was to pray for His persecutors (Isaiah 53:12; Luke 23:34)*

- *The people were to shake their heads at Him (Psalm 22:7; Mt. 27:39)*
- *The people were to ridicule Him (Psalm 22:17; Luke 23:35)*
- *His garments to be parted and lots cast (Psalm 22:18; John 19:24)*
- *His cry from the cross (Psalm 22:1; Matthew 27:46)*
- *His bones were not to be broken (Psalm 34:20; John 19:33, 36)*
- *His side pierced (Zechariah 12:10; John 19:34-37)*
- *Buried in a rich man's tomb (Isaiah 53:9; Matthew 27:57-60)*

Here are some from His birth and life:

- *pre-existence (Micah 5:2, John 1:1,14)*
- *God would provide Himself a lamb as an offering (Genesis 22:8; John 1:29)*
- *From the tribe of Judah (Genesis 49:10; Matthew 1:1-3)*
- *Heir to the throne of David (Isaiah 9:6-7; Matthew 1:1)*
- *Called "the Mighty God, The everlasting Father" (Isaiah 9:6; Matt 1:23)*
- *Born in Bethlehem (Micah 5:2; Matthew 2:1)*
- *Born of a Virgin (Isaiah 7:14; Matthew 1:18)*
- *Declared to be the Son of God (Psalm 2:7; Matthew 3:17)*
- *Called out of Egypt (Hosea 11:1; Matthew 2:15)*

- Would be a Nazarene (Judges 13:5; Amos 2:11; Lamentations 4:7; Matthew 2:23)
- Presented with gifts (Psalm 72:10; Matthew 2:1,11)
- He entered Jerusalem as a King riding on a donkey's colt (Zechariah 9:9; Matthew 21:5)
- Resurrected from the dead (Psalm 16:10-11; 49:15; Mark 16:6)
- Ascended to the right hand of God (Psalm 68:18; Luke 24:51)
- His coming in glory (Malachi 3:2-3, Luke 3:17)

Amazing, isn't it? Did you happen to notice how many different authors God used to share these very consistent prophesies? I think it is important to note that when David and Isaiah described crucifixion nearly 700 and 1,000 years respectively before Jesus Christ was born, it was an unknown method of execution. In their days stoning was the primary method of execution, so no broken bones would have been a big deal. Crucifixion described as "death on a tree" was not introduced until hundreds of years after their deaths. God is Sovereign! I challenge you to check out these verses for yourself. We will be exploring some of them in the life application section at the end of this chapter.

Do your Homework

Former atheist Lee Strobel did his homework. He set out to disprove Christianity and it led to his salvation. In his book, *The Case for Christ: A Journalist's Personal Investigation of the Evidence for Jesus*,[12] Lee shares his journey and the findings that led him to that conclusion. He studied historical records, biographical data, archeological records and psychological evidence that examined statements in the Bible about Jesus' life, ministry and resurrection. Strobel's research led him to the conclusion that Jesus was who He said He was; The Messiah and the incarnate Son of God who was raised from the dead.

Here is what Lee Strobel had to say about his journey to Jesus and the transformational experience of writing his book. Before the journey:

> "To be honest, I didn't want to believe that Christianity could radically transform someone's character and values. It was much easier to raise doubts and manufacture outrageous objections than to consider the possibility that God actually could trigger a revolutionary turn-around in such a depraved and degenerate life."[13]

The reason that he set his sails for this exploration:

> "I saw the positive changes in my wife. I never heard the real message of Christ before and didn't believe. But if it's true, this would have huge implications for my life."[14]

His decision for Christ after two years of research:

> "In short, I didn't become a Christian because God promised I would have an even happier life than I had as an atheist. He never promised any such thing. Indeed, following Him would inevitably bring divine demotions in the eyes of the world. Rather, I became a Christian because the evidence was so compelling that Jesus really is the one-

and-only Son of God who proved His divinity by rising from the dead. That meant following Him was the most rational and logical step I could possibly take."[15]

His transformation:

> "Sure enough, over time as I endeavored to follow Jesus' teachings, and open myself to His transforming power, my priorities, my values, my character were (and continue to be) gradually changed ... In fact, so radical was the difference in my life that a few months after I became a follower of Jesus, our five-year-old daughter Alison went up to my wife and said, 'Mommy, I want God to do for me what He has done for Daddy.' ... "Here was a little girl who had only known a father who was profane, angry, verbally harsh, and all too often absent. And even though she had never interviewed a scholar, never analyzed the data, never investigated historical evidence, she has seen up close the influences that Jesus can have on a person's life. In effect, she was saying, 'If this is what God does to a human being, that's what I want for me."[16]

That's what it is all about really. God's transformational love can be seen by others and it can be contagious! I encourage you to read *The Case for Christ: A Journalist's Personal Investigation of the Evidence for Jesus* by Lee Strobel. It really is amazing to see how reliable the Word of God is through the eyes of someone that was trying to disprove it. Since his salvation in 1981, Pastor, Doctor of Divinity and best-selling Author Lee Strobel's ministry has impacted millions of people with his more than 20 books, discipleship programs and his national TV program, *Faith Under Fire*. God is using this former atheist to grow the faith of millions. Learn more about Lee Strobel from his website www.LeeStrobel.com.

Former agnostic Josh McDowell went on a similar quest when he was in college. In response to his mocking their faith, student believers challenged Josh; if he could disprove the resurrection, they would all denounce Christ. In fact, if he could do that, the entire foundation of Christianity would crumble. Josh took that challenge to heart and began a journey that led him across the world to study as many original documents related to the Bible claims of the resurrection that he could find. He too set out on a serious mission to disprove Christianity. His exhaustive interviews and studies led him to the same conclusion as Lee Strobel. Jesus Christ was who He claimed to be: the resurrected living Son of God.

At the age of 20, Josh responded to an altar call that changed his life forever. Speaking of that moment of his salvation decision in his short book, *My Journey...From Skepticism to Faith*, Josh says, *"But it wasn't the evidence for Christ's resurrection that made me break into a cold sweat that autumn evening in Factoryville, Michigan. It was something else. It was God's love. His unmistakable, obsessive love for me, a sinner! The truth only made my head swim."*[17]

Since that fateful day in the fall of 1960, Josh has been busy serving the King of Kings. Here is just a sampling from his resumé found on his website www.Josh.org. He has written or co-authored 138 books including, *More Than a Carpenter* which has sold more than 15 million copies in 85 languages and *New*

Evidence That Demands a Verdict which was named by World Magazine as one the twentieth century's top 40 books and one of the 13 most influential books of the last 50 years on Christian thought.

As a well-known speaker, Josh has addressed more than 25 million people, giving over 26,000 talks in 125 countries. Now that is kingdom impact motivated by the love of Christ! We will touch a bit more on Josh McDowell's amazing story with a clip from *Undaunted: the Early Life of Josh McDowell* later in this book.

I don't know about you, but I am grateful that men like Henry Liddon, Peter Stoner, Lee Strobel and Josh McDowell did their homework. You and I can read their books and read the Bible and see for ourselves and I hope that you will. Jesus is alive and well on planet earth today. He is changing lives and He can change yours, too. These were ordinary men who allowed their hearts to surrender to God's love and they allowed God to use them in miraculous ways. He can do the same thing in your life!

You Need HIM: Clip from Fireproof

Fireproof

http://bit.ly/15EOJGC [18]

See PattySadallah.com Other Books tab Paperback Film Links, Fireproof

Can you relate to Caleb at the beginning of this clip from *Fireproof*? Just about everyone has been in a lopsided relationship like this one. One person tries more or seems to care more than the other person. At least one or both people involved in those types of relationships are stubborn, self-centered and ungrateful. Caleb wanted out. He was getting tired of the lack of response from his efforts. Our human tendency in cases like these is to run for our lives. It's painful and exhausting to live with this kind of rejection.

I am so glad that God has more patience with me than I have with others. The Lord loves us unconditionally regardless of how much we reject Him. "How am I supposed to show love to someone over and over and over who constantly rejects me?" Seeing this question of Caleb's through God's eyes really puts things in perspective.

God is Love

God showed His ultimate love for us by dying on the cross.

1 John 4:7-8, "Beloved, let us love one another, for love is from God, and whoever loves has been born of God and knows God. Anyone who does not love does not know God, because God is love."

We get our ability to love from God

One of my favorite parts of this clip is when Caleb's dad makes it clear that love is a choice. It is not a feeling, it's a deliberate action. The key is the motivation behind the love. "I have made a decision to love your mother whether she deserves it or not." God loves you even though you don't deserve it and even in the face of rejection. He can't help Himself. It's His nature to love us.

Caleb wanted to fix his wife. Can you relate to that one too? We all do that, don't we? We can't see our role in the problem, but we can so clearly see what the other person is doing wrong. God can't do anything wrong; He is perfect. So, if something is messed up in our lives, we have some measure of responsibility to take for it.

I learned this one in my own marriage. I once heard a professor from a communication class in college say that all anger is unmet expectations. We expect people to behave a certain way and when they don't, it makes us angry. I used to be angry that George didn't behave the way I expected; he used to be angry that I didn't behave according to his expectations and it drew us farther and farther apart. Jesus confronted me with this and basically told me to worry about myself and my relationship with Him and it softened my heart for George. I stopped trying to fix him and he responded in kind.

My Grammy was a very wise woman. She only had an eighth-grade education, but she was one of the wisest women I have ever met. I would sit near her when she was baking or ironing and take in her wisdom like a sponge. I can remember one of our talks on the eve of my wedding day. She told me that the secret to a strong and happy marriage was to give more than you ever expected to receive. Service was the ultimate love language and if you put other people's needs ahead of your own, you will reap rewards beyond your imagination. Something wonderful happens in your heart when you give, she would say, and when you receive something from someone out of service and love, your heart wants to give back. This is the power of reciprocity.

Jesus Changes Lives

Decide to love others by choosing first to love God. God is the wellspring of love. The more we spend time getting to know God, the more His love will pour into us. The more love that pours into us, the more we can make the choice to love others. Jesus changes lives. If your life isn't changed by Jesus, you don't know Him yet. It is impossible to encounter Jesus and not be changed. Jesus will give you a greater capacity to love if you choose Him.

If you think you are saved and have not been changed by Jesus, it's time to ask Him for a fresh encounter. Jesus wants to change you and He can heal any relationship. He can make you less stubborn, less selfish and more grateful. Remember what we have already said about the Fruit of the Spirit? *"The fruit of the Holy Spirit produces this kind of fruit in our lives: love, joy, peace, patience, kindness, goodness, faithfulness, gentleness, and self-control. There is no law against these things!" ~ Galatians 5:22-23*

Everything on that list is yours. Just pray for it and stop trying to be those things in your own strength. We can't have those characteristics in our life without God because they are gifts from God.

This next portion is between you and the Lord. But I love you too much to not tell you the truth.

Free Ticket

Imagine that a man offered you a choice between two free tickets for a future one-way trip at an unknown time in the future.

"Take your time and do your homework on these tickets before you choose," the guy told you. You are a very busy person and, since this thing will happen at an unknown time in the future, you figured it wasn't that important. You didn't know when it would be or what the destinations were, so you didn't bother to investigate the difference between the two tickets. You figured that they were free, so it didn't make much difference, so you grabbed one of the tickets.

The time finally came for you to go on your trip. Your plane ticket was to go to a stinky, mosquito ridden swamp. Nasty swamps and bug bites are not your cup of tea. You wondered what the other ticket destination was, so you decided to head back to the airport to check out the other destination.

You learned that the other option was a ticket to paradise. So you head back to the airport counter and hand the ticket agent your swamp ticket. They look at your ticket and say, "Sorry, but this ticket is for the swamp. I need the ticket to paradise. You need the right ticket to get on this flight."

Are you going to get mad at that guy for not letting you on that plane? Both tickets were free. You had the chance to research the difference between the two tickets before you took them. But you chose not to bother. I mean, everyone knows that a ticket to paradise is better than a ticket to a swamp, right? Wouldn't you have chosen the paradise tickets if you realized how much better they were? Of course, you would.

God offers you a free ticket to heaven; which by the way is indescribably better than any place we call "paradise" on Earth. People choose the alternative every day just because they don't do their homework.

What does the Bible say about heaven? For those who choose the ticket to Heaven, here is a bit of what that will be like:

> *Revelation 21:1-4*
>
> *"¹Then I saw "a new heaven and a new earth,"[a] for the first heaven and the first earth had passed away, and there was no longer any sea. ² I saw the Holy City, the new Jerusalem, coming down out of heaven from God, prepared as a bride beautifully dressed for her husband. ³ And I heard a loud voice from the throne saying, "Look! God's dwelling place is now among the people, and He will dwell with them. They will be His people, and God Himself will be with them and be their God. ⁴ 'He will wipe every tear from their eyes. There will be no more death'[b] or mourning or crying or pain, for the old order of things has passed away."*
>
> *Revelation 21:18-21*
>
> *¹⁸ "The wall was made of jasper, and the city of pure gold, as pure as glass. ¹⁹ The foundations of the city walls were decorated with every kind of*

> *precious stone. The first foundation was jasper, the second sapphire, the third agate, the fourth emerald, [20] the fifth onyx, the sixth ruby, the seventh chrysolite, the eighth beryl, the ninth topaz, the tenth turquoise, the eleventh jacinth, and the twelfth amethyst.[] 21 The twelve gates were twelve pearls, each gate made of a single pearl. The great street of the city was of gold, as pure as transparent glass."*

Hell is real. We know it's real because God told us about it in the Bible. *Revelation 20:13 (MSG), "I saw a Great White Throne and the One Enthroned. Nothing could stand before or against the Presence, nothing in Heaven, nothing on earth. And then I saw all the dead, great and small, standing there—before the Throne! And books were opened. Then another book was opened: The Book of Life. The dead were judged by what was written in the books; by the way they had lived. Sea released its dead, Death and Hell turned in their dead. Each man and woman was judged by the way he or she had lived. Then Death and Hell were hurled into Lake Fire. This is the second death—Lake Fire. Anyone whose name was not found inscribed in the Book of Life was hurled into Lake Fire."*

Hell is the other ticket; the one that most people choose because they don't do their homework. God doesn't send people to hell, people choose hell. God went out of His way to warn us about hell by sending His Son to teach us how to avoid it. He even paid the price for us to not have to go there. The good news is that we don't need to be perfect to avoid hell. We just need to accept that free ticket.

Revelation 1:7-8

₇ "Look, He is coming with the clouds, [b]

and "every eye will see Him,

even those who pierced Him";

and all peoples on earth will mourn because of Him.[c]

So shall it be! Amen.

₈ "I am the Alpha and the Omega," says the Lord God, "who is, and who was, and who is to come, the Almighty."

These verses describe a future when everyone who has ever been born will see Jesus — regardless of whether you believed in Him or not while you were on this planet. That's the day you will want to make sure you chose the right ticket!

God's gift of grace is your free plane ticket to Heaven. This benefit in not for you to redeem only when you die. God sends the Holy Spirit to live in your heart the moment you accept that free ticket. He is there, sealed in your heart forever. He is there to help you live the abundant life each day you draw breath.

How do I know that God wants YOU? Because:

*John 3:16, "For God loved the world so much that He gave His one and only Son, so that **everyone** who believes in Him will not perish but have eternal life."*

Why hasn't God returned already?

> *2 Peter 3:9* says *"The Lord isn't really being slow about His promise, as some people think. No, He is being **patient** for your sake. **He does not want anyone to be destroyed but wants everyone to repent.**"* *(bold emphasis mine)*

The coolest part of the Christian life is that He is with you always. The more time you spend with God the more you can "feel" His presence, the more you can "see" Him working, the more you can "hear" His voice. God is real and the more you believe Him, not just believe His existence, but *really believe* what He tells you about Himself in the Bible, the more your life will be transformed.

Regardless of whether you believed in Him or not while you were on this planet, we all die one day. That's the day you will want to make sure you chose the right ticket!

Let's summarize. You can spend eternity with streets of gold, no tears, perfect love, and perfect health by simply accepting God's gift of grace. Or, you can ignore God. "Every eye will see" means you and I will see Jesus when He comes back in the clouds. That's when your choice on Earth will be so important. Which ticket do you have right now? As long as you are still here on Earth, there is still time to get the better ticket!

What the Father Did for You: Clip from Most- The Bridge

Most (Czech for 'The Bridge') is a beautiful Oscar-nominated movie and winner of many prestigious film festivals. It tells the story of the close relationship between a bridge operator and his young son, and the fateful day when both try to avoid an impending rail disaster.

Bridge

http://bit.ly/GReYTO [19]

See PattySadallah.com Other Books tab Paperback Film Links, Bridge

Did you notice that the hundreds of passengers on that steam train were completely unaware of the danger as they proceeded towards an open drawbridge? They had no idea of the horrible decision this father had to make in order to save them. Isn't that just like us? God the Father sacrificed His only Son for us and we are either unaware or unappreciative of the sacrifice.

This heart-wrenching story, which portrays the greatest measure of love, sacrifice, hope and forgiveness, is a perfect metaphor for what the Father and Jesus did for us. In this clip, the son and the father both wanted to save the people on the train. They both willingly made painful sacrifices toward that greater good.

Who crucified Jesus? Was it the Sadducees, the Religious leaders of the day, who plotted to kill Jesus? Or was it Judas the disloyal disciple, when he betrayed Jesus for 30 pieces of silver? Was it the crowd that demanded His crucifixion? Can we blame King Herod or Pontius Pilate? Surely, they were in positions of authority to stop the crucifixion.

If it's finger-pointing we desire, then point a finger at me and you. Did we crucify Jesus? Our sins necessitated His sacrifice. Actually, it was God Himself that allowed Jesus's crucifixion and used it as the very mechanism to bring us into His presence. It was Jesus's willingness to do the will of the Holy Father that bridged the gap for you and me to be saved.

> *John 15:13 "Greater love has no one than this that he lay down his life for his friends."*

Jesus willingly gave His life for you and me. It wasn't the Jewish leaders, Pontius Pilate or Judas or the crowd that sent Jesus to the cross. It was all part of God's perfect plan to open the gates of heaven for us. Jesus chose to die so He could save us. The Heavenly Father could have saved His Son from that fate, but He knew it was in our best interest to let Him die.

> *Philippians 2:3-11 "Do nothing out of selfish ambition or vain conceit. Rather, in humility value others above yourselves, $_4$ not looking to your own interests, but each of you to the interests of the others. $_5$ In your relationships with one another, have the same mindset as Christ Jesus: $_6$ Who ,being in very nature]a] God, did not consider equality with God something to be used to His own advantage; $_7$ rather, He made Himself nothing, by taking the very nature[b] of a servant, being made in human*

> likeness. ₈ *And being found in appearance as a man, He humbled Himself by becoming obedient to death—even death on a cross!* ₉ *Therefore God exalted Him to the highest place and gave Him the name that is above every name,* ₁₀ *that at the name of Jesus every knee should bow, in heaven and on earth and under the earth,* ₁₁ *and every tongue acknowledge that Jesus Christ is Lord, to the glory of God the Father."*

That, my friend, is the definition of love.

Think about it for a second. The Very God, the Creator of the Universe chose to humble Himself to become human. While on Earth, He taught us how to live and love. Then He willingly laid down His life to die on the cross as the Perfect Lamb for our sins so that we could have eternal life and fellowship with Him in heaven. In doing so, Jesus gave us the gift of eternal salvation, freedom from all strongholds, power to overcome any challenge, the peace that is beyond understanding, and the ability to have Him with us every moment of the day. You have the God of the universe, who knows your name and cares about the big and the small of your life sealed in your heart, with you every day. What an incomparable gift!

So, what can you give Jesus in return? I think the answers are in verses above. Humble yourself. Do nothing with selfish motives. Put others' needs ahead of yours. Basically, learn to be and live more like Jesus every day. I don't know about you, but if I just reflect a bit on what God has done for me, I could spend a lifetime thanking Him in these ways and it wouldn't be enough.

> *1 John 4:8 says, "Whoever does not love does not know God, because God is love." And 1 John 4:16, "And so we know and rely on the love God has for us. God is love. Whoever lives in love lives in God, and God in them."*

God is love, love is good, and therefore God is good. What does God have to say about Love?

> *1 Corinthians 13*
>
> *"₁ If I speak in the tongues[a] of men or of angels, but do not have love, I am only a resounding gong or a clanging cymbal. ₂ If I have the gift of prophecy and can fathom all mysteries and all knowledge, and if I have a faith that can move mountains, but do not have love, I am nothing. ₃ If I give all I possess to the poor and give over my body to hardship that I may boast,[b] but do not have love, I gain nothing.*
>
> *₄ Love is patient, love is kind. It does not envy, it does not boast, it is not proud. ₅ It does not dishonor others, it is not self-seeking, it is not easily angered, it keeps no record of wrongs. ₆ Love does not delight in evil but rejoices with the truth. ₇ It always protects, always trusts, always hopes, always perseveres.*
>
> *₈ Love never fails. But where there are prophecies, they will cease; where there are tongues, they will be stilled; where there is knowledge, it will pass away. ₉ For we know in part and we prophesy in part, ₁₀ but when completeness comes, what is in*

part disappears. ₁₁ When I was a child, I talked like a child, I thought like a child, I reasoned like a child. When I became a man, I put the ways of childhood behind me. ₁₂ For now we see only a reflection as in a mirror; then we shall see face to face. Now I know in part; then I shall know fully, even as I am fully known.

₁₃ And now these three remain: faith, hope and love. But the greatest of these is love."

Love is a choice. It's not a just an emotional feeling. Did you see the action words in these verses? Love is faith with feet! It implies selfless behavior. We are by nature selfish human beings. Selfishness is part of our survival instincts. Look at babies. They scream or cry to indicate that they need something.

We can't be or behave selflessly without God. We can't be any of the things in these verses above without God. Jesus was the only one who lived out this kind of love perfectly. But we can be transformed to live this kind of love life too, if we let God in and trust Him to change us.

Jesus, God's only Son, who was 100% God and 100% man, lived a sinless life on this earth. He showed us God's heart and intentions for us. He willingly laid down His life so that you and I could be forgiven. He was raised from the dead, sent the Holy Spirit to live in the hearts of every single person who accepts Him and He will stand in the gap for you and me on Judgment Day. So that when God looks at your life, every word and decision you have made, every mistake, every wrong turn, the Father sees only Jesus's perfection and He lets us into Heaven.

Salvation Prayer

You don't need to say specific words. You don't need to be on your knees or say words with your eyes closed. This is not an intellectual process. This is a decision of the heart. If you are truly ready to receive Jesus or if you would like to help someone else receive Jesus here is a sample prayer that you can use to do this.

Lord Jesus, I need you. I know that I am a sinner and can never be perfect enough to get to Heaven on my own. Thank You for dying on the cross and paying the price for my sins. Thank you for rising from the dead and making a way for me to join you in heaven.

Thank you for forgiving me of my sins. Thank you for this loving sacrifice for me.

I believe you are the Way, the Truth, and the Life. I believe you are the only way to Heaven, the only way to the Father. And right now, as an act of my will, by faith and trust in you, I open the door of my heart and my life and receive you as my Savior and Lord. Help mold me into your character and give me the abundant Christian life.

Thank you for giving me the gift of eternal life in heaven! Please Jesus, take control of my life right now and have mercy on me. Show me your will. Teach me your Word. Guide me by your Holy Spirit.

Take the throne of my life, Lord Jesus, and make me the kind of person you want me to be. In the holy and precious name of Jesus, I pray. Amen.

If you are sincere about what you just prayed, right now open your Bible to John 6:47 (AMP) and see what Jesus says about what you have just received!

"I tell you the truth, he (you) who believes has (starting right now) everlasting life."

This means God has just forgiven your sins and given you the gift of eternal life in heaven! Until the day you arrive in heaven, Jesus has sent the Holy Spirit to live in your heart to help guide and direct your life so you can overcome all things through Jesus's strength!

If you have just read the salvation prayer, let us know so we can send you a support gift. Email Patty@PattySadallah.com . Welcome to God's Family!

Life Application: BEGIN CENTER

1. What is the number one area of your life that you would like to see transformed by the power of the Holy Spirit?

2. Look up any two pairs of Prophetic Proof Scriptures from page 42-44. What did you learn about the relationship between the Old and New Testament scriptures? What surprised you the most about those statistics?

3. Have you or do you know someone who has been personally transformed by the love of Christ? How are you/they different today than before being saved?

4. Can you relate to Caleb in the *Fireproof* clip? Have you ever felt like you were in a one-way relationship? We can't out love God but, how may you love Him better than you do currently?

5. If you were to die today, which ticket would you have? Reflect on your answer.

6. What did you learn about God from the Bridge clip? Share any insights that you may have received from that clip related to God's sacrifice for you.

NORTH
Grow Your Relationship with Christ

How do you fall in love with Jesus and let Him transform you? Just like if you are falling in love with a person, you would spend time to get to know them. In this chapter we will address the living Word of God and how to pray more effectively so that you can see miracles and transformation in your own life.

The Bible- God's Love Story & Mouthpiece

Even though the Bible contains 66 books written by more than 40 authors over more than 1,000 years, it is ONE love story. Pastor Jonathan Schaeffer summarized this fact in one sermon. He broke it down into five acts as if it were a play. Below is an adaptation from Pastor Jonathan Schaeffer's sermon notes.[20]

- **Act 1: Creation—God reaches out to people in friendship *(Genesis 1-2)***

    God creates a perfect environment for the people He's made. Best of all, He gifts them with His presence and friendship. There is direct access to God in the Garden of Eden so they can fellowship with God freely.

- **Act 2: The Fall —The friendship is shattered due to sin *(Genesis 3-11)***

God gave Adam and Eve free will because He wanted them to choose to love Him back. Adam and Eve choose to walk away from God; sin infects them, all of their descendants . . . and the introduction of sin wreaks havoc in the whole world. This affects everyone born after them.

- **Act 3: Israel—God builds a nation *(Genesis 12-Malachi)***

Launching a plan to restore the broken friendship, God chooses to bless childless Abraham, making him the father of a great nation—Israel—and using this nation as a blessing to the world. A Jewish Savior is promised who will remove the curse of sin.

- **Act 4: Jesus—A Savior restores the friendship *(Matthew-John)***

Jesus is Immanuel, "God with us," who fulfills the promises of the Old Testament and reverses the curse of sin by dying a cruel death. He is the central figure in the story, finally restoring the friendship God always intended with the people He created.

- **Act 5: God's new family—purpose for today & forever *(Acts-Revelation)***

God's Spirit comes to live in those who follow Jesus, forming a new community who will show His love to people of every nation. What was the goal? Jesus wants everyone to be saved and to understand the truth and He gave His life to purchase freedom for everyone." *(1 Timothy 2:4, 7)*

The entire point of even creating people was so that we could have a relationship with our God.

In addition to being a love story, the Bible is the living Word of God. *Hebrews 4:12, "For the word of God is alive and active. Sharper than any double-edged sword, it penetrates even to dividing soul and spirit, joints and marrow; it judges the thoughts and attitudes of the heart."*

How is the Bible the living Word of God? The words are the same from one Bible to another; It's not like the words change every day. There are lots of versions that use different words to say the same thing and help people understand better. But all have been anointed by God so there is no deviation from one to another. That makes the Bible stable and reliable. But how was it a living document?

Christians have the Holy Spirit living in our hearts. When we read or pray the Bible, the Holy Spirit interacts with us. He causes words or phrases to pop off the page and make sense to us for the exact need and circumstance each time. I have a dog-eared Bible that I have underlined and written all over. I can pick up that Bible and a verse that I had never underlined or commented about will pop up in that moment and be exactly what I needed. Likewise, I can reread a section that I made comments and the notes all over and it just doesn't speak to me today like it did then. The combination of the written word of God and the Holy Spirit brings the Bible to life for each believer.

I love to pick up my Bible, pray that God would lead me to exactly what I need from Him, close my eyes and open the book. My eyes will go to the exact verse that God wants me to read and pray. This practice ministers to me every time. I can remember my first year as a Christian, after reading through the book of John; I read the Bible like that every day for months. It was a great way to grow my faith and understanding.

God desires a two-way relationship. He speaks to us through the Bible with the aid of the Holy Spirit for understanding. We speak to Him through prayer. Jesus sent the Holy Spirit so that we could understand God more easily. If you pick up some scripture verses and don't understand them, ask God to make it clear. When we pray scriptures back to God, we can be confident that our prayers are according to His will and know He will answer them. Praying back scriptures are prayers that are always according to God's will so you know that He will answer them.

Identity in Christ: Identity Clip

Perhaps one of the most critical secrets to living the abundant Christian life is to get a clear and accurate view of who God is and who you are in Christ. Why is that so critically important? When we limit God in our own minds by putting human constraints on what He can do, we fall into the trap of the enemy.

Identity

http://bit.ly/2GH1␣i01 [21]

See PattySadallah.com Other Books tab Paperback Film Links, Identity

This clip sheds light on so many important aspects of Christian identity. It begins with people identifying themselves with their jobs. You are not your career. The danger of identifying yourself this way is that the world puts different values on different roles that people play in society. God does not look at you through this lens. When for example, a stay at home mom introduces herself as "just a homemaker", I believe it grieves the Holy Spirit. Nobody is "just" anything. Not only is it an honorable choice, but the Lord loves people equally, regardless of what they do. Do not let society tell you otherwise.

Then the clip transitions into negative self-identity statements. Whenever you use the words "I am" in a sentence you are making a statement about how you see yourself. Never speak an "I am" sentence that is negative- ever. When you do you are agreeing with the enemy and compromising God's best for you.

One of the most revealing lessons I learned in my doctoral program is that words are subject to sowing and reaping. The Lord spoke the universe into existence by speaking words. We are created in His image and therefore our words have power as well.

Statements like: "I am an alcoholic," "I am a drug addict," "I am a failure," "I am a victim," "I will always be fat because it runs in my family" are declarations of your faith in negative things. Out of the mouth the heart speaks. There are 27 Bible verses that warn of this very thing. When you say something like "I always struggle with money," you will always struggle with money! This is because first you had to think it, then your heart believes it which leads you to expect it. When you speak it out loud, you activate that very thing to happen in your life. Your mouth waters the seed. This is the nature of the law of sowing and reaping. Sow Biblical truth by your thoughts and words and you will reap the promised blessings in the Bible. Speak the lies of the enemy, and you will reap the curses of the enemy.

Did you notice the contrast between the limiting lies of who we think we are or what other people can say we are, versus the empowering truth of who we actually are in Christ? I loved how even the posture and attitudes of the people in the clip changed as they spoke about the empowering truth of who they are in Christ. Knowing in our heads and believing in our hearts the truth about who God is gives us a higher view of God and an empowering view of ourselves. When we know and believe God for who He says He is, then it is easier for us to have faith.

Our view of God should be very high. God is higher that we will ever understand. When we think of God as merely human and limit what He can do in our own minds, we are robbing ourselves of a faith that can move mountains. Jesus was 100% God AND 100% man. It's hard to wrap our heads around that one. But, if God was small enough to fit inside our puny brains, He wouldn't be God!

Believing God for His promises is critical to living in victory. Remember, if you are saved, Satan can't steal your salvation, but he can steal your impact, so you want to cling on to the Truth of God and Satan will flee.

> *James 4:6-10, "But He gives us more grace. That is why Scripture says 'God opposes the proud but shows favor to the humble. [c]'*

> *⁷ Submit yourselves, then, to God. Resist the devil, and he will flee from you. ⁸ Come near to God and He will come near to you. Wash your hands, you sinners, and purify your hearts, you double-minded. ⁹ Grieve, mourn and wail. Change your laughter to mourning and your joy to gloom. ¹⁰ Humble yourselves before the Lord, and He will lift you up."*

Did you catch how important humility is for success against the enemy? We want to have a right view of God and a right view of ourselves. Our self-view should be moderate — not too high and not too low. An exaggerated high view of one's self leads to pride and arrogance. *Proverbs 16:18* warns, *"Pride goes before destruction, and a haughty spirit before a fall."*

Spending time meditating on the characteristics of God will help you remember who God is when you need Him. Memorizing key scriptures is a great practice. Jesus's Disciple John truly understood the importance of knowing who God is. If you have never picked up a Bible, start with John. Here are just a few verses to reflect on, pray through and memorize from the books of John and 1 John:

- *1 John 4:8 (ESV) "Anyone who does not love does not know God, because God is love."*

- *John 14:6 (ESV), "Jesus said to Him, "I am the way, and the truth, and the life. No one comes to the Father except through me."*

- *1 John 1:5 (ESV), "This is the message we have heard from Him and proclaim to you, that God is light, and in Him is no darkness at all."*

- *John 3:16 (ESV), "For God so loved the world, that He gave*

> His only Son, that whoever believes in Him should not perish but have eternal life."

- 1 John 4:14 (ESV), "And we have seen and testify that the Father has sent His Son to be the Savior of the world."

What Jesus had to say about the mustard seed:

No one was more zealous about the 30-day faith challenge I recently issued than Dr. Anthony "Doc" Raimondo. The group was challenged to ask for God to increase the gift of faith in their heart several times a day for 30 days. The hypothesis was that if the gift of faith (One of the Holy Spirit Manifestation gifts we will talk about in the East Chapter) was increased, there would be an increase in other Holy Spirit manifestation gifts as well. The hypothesis proved true with participants sharing lots of life-altering stories, signs, wonders, miracles, freedom and breakthroughs. Doc took this challenge so seriously that he experienced so many Jesus encounters and miracles in that month that he cataloged them in a daily log!

One of Doc's Jesus experiences was related to the mustard seed. An effective Bible meditation exercise I learned at CLU was to ask Jesus to take me to a Bible scene in the spirit and explain it to me. This is one of the most amazing Jesus encountering exercises you can ever put into practice.

My friend Doc was reading the story about the conversation Jesus had with His disciples about the mustard seed in Matthew 13. He was meditating on this verse and had a vision of himself on the road with Jesus and His disciples when He picked up a tiny mustard seed on the ground and spoke to them about the size of the seed. But Jesus didn't stop there in Doc's vision.

Jesus said; *"But do you know why this tiny seed grows in to a mighty tree? "*

"Why Lord?" The disciples asked.

Jesus answered; *"Because it knows Whose it is, and what it is created to become. It simply evolves in pursuit of what the Father designed it to be."*

The Father sees us through Jesus's perfection. When we agree with God for the truth of how He sees us, we are free to evolve in pursuit of how he sees us already. The person that God has planned for you to become is at the center of the issue of your core identity. It is your "Christ Identity." At CLU we refer to this as the Christ-I. The journey to the abundant Christian life essentially is discovering and agreeing with God about your Christ-I. Your Christ-I is the sweet aroma of Jesus's perfection mixed with the uniqueness of your one and only self.

I have one more critically important point related to your Christ-I. We've already learned that the Father sees you through Jesus's perfection. The startling thing is that the enemy sees you the way you see yourself. For example, if you see yourself as a weak victim, you have a bulls-eye on your back inviting spiritual warfare. But when you agree with God about who you are in Christ, the enemy will be afraid of you because when you walk in the room, they see Jesus walking into the room. This is a true picture for the new covenant believer. I love this quote from Graham Cooke in his book *The Nature of Freedom: Letters from God Series Book One:* "When you realize who you are in Him and who He is for you, that oneness and unity breaks every power against you."

I've written much more about this Bible exercise and shared

more Jesus encountering revelations about Bible stories in *How to Live a Worry Free Life: Just Asked Jesus Series Book 1*.

The Praise Alphabet

Instead of counting sheep, I like to list the praise worthy attributes of God or thank Him for the many truths that I have in Christ. You can do this exercise yourself too; it's a great way to get in touch with who God is and who you are in Christ. This is not an all-inclusive list, so you can add your own to it. But I hope you like the ones that I have for you today in this example of both who God is and who we are in Christ:

- God is the **A**ncient of Days, **A**lmighty God, and we are His **A**dopted **A**mbassadors and we are **A**dored;

- God is the **B**read of Life, and the **B**right Morning Star, and we are **B**lameless, **B**lessed, **B**ranches and His **B**eloved;

- God is the **C**reator, **C**hrist, the **C**omforter, **C**ounselor and **C**aretaker and We are His **C**hosen **C**hildren, and **C**o-heirs with **C**hrist, and we are **C**alled for a specific purpose;

- God is the **D**oor, **D**ivine, the **D**eliverer and the **D**efender of the weak, and we are **D**elivered;

- God is the **E**verlasting, **E**ternal King, and we are **E**ternally kept in the palm of His hand, have **E**ternal Life, and we are **E**mpowered by the Holy Spirit to bear much fruit;

- God is the Heavenly **F**ather, **F**aithful, the **F**ount of Life, and we are **F**orgiven, **F**ree and **F**aithful;

- God is the only **G**od, the **G**reat Physician, the **G**ate, the **G**ift Giver, **G**reat High Priest and **G**lory of the Lord, and we are **G**rateful and **G**rowing in our faith;

- God is the **H**oly Spirit and **H**ealer, and we are **H**umbled and **H**eaven- bound thanks to His Sacrifice;
- God is the Great **I** Am, the **I**mage of God, **I**mmanuel, and we are His **I**nheritance;
- God is **J**esus, **J**ust and **J**udge, and we are **J**ustified;
- God is the **K**ing of **K**ings and **K**ind, and we are **K**ept from the evil one;
- God is the **L**amb of God, **L**ove, **L**awgiver, the **L**ight of the World and the **L**ord of **L**ords, and we are **L**oved;
- God is the **M**essiah, **M**erciful, **M**ighty to Save and **M**ajestic, and we are **M**inisters of the Word;
- God is **N**ear and **N**ever changing, and we are **N**ever alone;
- God is **O**mnipotent, **O**mnipresent, **O**mniscient, the **O**nly begotten Son, and we are **O**ver-comers;
- God is the **P**rince of **P**eace and **P**atient, and we are **P**recious **P**ossessions and have the **P**ower of the Holy Spirit living within us;
- God is the **Q**uiet Still Voice and **Q**uintessential, and we are **Q**uickened by His mighty power;
- God is **R**uler, the **R**ighteous **R**edeemer, and we are **R**econciled and **R**edeemed and part of the **R**oyal family;
- God is the **S**on of God, **S**avior, **S**ufficient, the Great **S**hepherd and **S**low to anger, and we are **S**et free, **S**aved, **S**ervants of the Most High God and **S**hepherds of His gifts and resources;

- God is **T**eacher, the **T**ruth and the Life, and we are His **T**emple and His **T**reasure;
- God is **U**nmatched and **U**nshakeable, and we are **U**nder His protection;
- God is **V**ictorious, the **V**ine, and we are His **V**essel and **V**ictorious over all strongholds;
- God is The **W**ay, The **W**ord, **W**isdom and **W**onderful, and we are **W**elcomed into His presence;
- God is e**X**traordinary, and we are e**X**traordinarily blessed;
- God is **Y**ahweh, and we need to **Y**ield to His will;
- God is **Z**ealous, **Z**ion's Ruler, and we are to serve Him with **Z**eal;

You can also just pick one or two of these characteristics and really meditate on what it means. Do you think that God being the Great Physician and Healer would help you cope with a chronic illness? Maybe you need wisdom for a challenging situation. God is Wisdom; ask Him for guidance. What if you are struggling with a habitual stronghold? Do you believe God when He says you have the power within you, by the Holy Spirit, to be victorious over all strongholds? If you did, would it help? Of course it would!

I hope you will meditate on these truths and practice your own Praise Alphabet exercise. You will be blessed by it!

Pray for Shrimp: Clip from Forrest Gump

God doesn't always answer our prayers exactly the way that we'd expect. In this clip from *Forrest Gump*, Lt. Dan was questioning Forrest's belief that God would provide them with shrimp.

Just as Lt. Dan was mocking God, "God showed up" with a mighty storm. During this horrible storm, Lt. Dan kept taunting and challenging God. All the while, God was protecting them and their shrimp boat. That fateful day was the beginning of a prosperous blessing for their business.

Pray for Shrimp

http://bit.ly/1dSdH8g [22]

PattySadallah.com Other Books tab Paperback Film Links, Pray for Shrimp

We don't always see what God's sovereign plan is for our lives; we can only claim the promises of God. According to *Joshua 1:5, "No one will be able to stand against you all the days of your life. As I was with Moses, so I will be with you; I will never leave you nor forsake you."*

If God feels far away, you moved. He is always right there. God's answers to your prayers are sometimes "yes," "no" or "not now." If He answers "no" to a prayer, God has a much bigger or better plan for you that we can't see from our view on Earth. We must trust that in the long run, things will work out for your own good. Answers of "no" are always for your own good because God's will is perfect.

If God answers, "not now," then there are likely other people, circumstances and pieces that are not yet ready, and the timing just isn't quite right. Often, we are simply not spiritually mature for the blessings that God has for us because our pride may creep in and steal God's glory.

If God answers yes, then the timing and our hearts are ready for the blessings that He has in the answered prayer.

One thing is for sure though, just like in this clip, God will likely answer your prayer differently than we expect. *Isaiah 55:8-9, "For my thoughts are not your thoughts, neither are your ways my ways,' declares the Lord. 'As the heavens are higher than the earth, so are my ways higher than your ways and my thoughts than your thoughts."*

We may never see the entire big picture, but we need to trust that God's will is perfect. We need to claim this verse and believe it as an absolute truth. *Jeremiah 29:11, "'For I know the plans I have for you," declares the Lord, "'plans to prosper you and not to harm you, plans to give you hope and a future."'*

Discerning God's Will

If praying God's will is the secret to an effective prayer life, then how do we know what God's will is?

> *Romans 12:2, "Do not conform to the pattern of this world but be transformed by the renewing of your mind. Then you will be able to test and approve what God's will is—His good, pleasing and perfect will."*

When it comes to decision-making, the pattern of this world tends to be exactly the opposite of how God makes decisions.

What do we tend to do? See if this problem-solving sequence resonates with you. When most of us are faced with a challenge, do we:

- Ask, "Have I encountered this problem before? How did I handle it in the past?"
- Ask our friends what they think.
- Maybe pray about the issue, but we pray for it to work out our way.
- Some of us may go to the Bible and see what God's Word has to say. Sadly, we often skip God's word entirely from the process.
- Then we make a decision and act on what we chose to do.

God's ways are so much wiser than our ways. We need to flip the order of those steps to make sure that we are making decisions according to God's perfect will.

When I worked as a Chapter President at Truth at Work, we used a Biblically-based decision-making model as a guide for our roundtable members.[23] This is the four-step model that will help you stay on God's track when you are making decisions:

1. First, go to God's Word,
2. Pray God's Word back to God.
3. Seek Godly Counsel.
4. Apply your personal experience and act.

Let's break these steps down to see how you would practically use this process. Think of a challenge or an opportunity that you are facing in your life. Maybe it's a problem with a co-worker or family member, an ethical dilemma at work, or a possible change in work or life circumstance that you want to seek God for guidance.

First go to God's Word. If you aren't sure how to go to God's Word for guidance, one of the easiest ways is to download a free toolbar on your computer from www.biblegateway.com or simply visit that website. This will let you search the Bible for keywords or themes, and it will pull up the appropriate scriptures. You can compare the same scriptures in a variety of Bible versions. You can read the whole chapter by clicking 'chapter.' These tips will help you better understand the Word as God intended it. You can also find Bible scholar commentaries on that site below the list of scriptures to see how others have interpreted them and made life applications.

Bible Gateway is not the only Bible site on the web. You can web search "Bible" to find others. If you are not web savvy, most Bibles have a concordance in the back that will do the same thing. A concordance is like an index by topic and keyword. If you can only remember that God called Himself the 'Bread of Life' and want to find that in the Bible, you can look in the concordance and find *John 6:35*.

> *"Then Jesus declared, I am the bread of life. Whoever comes to me will never go hungry, and whoever believes in me will never be thirsty"*

Once you have found helpful scriptures, pray them back to

God. Why is that important and how do you pray back scripture to God? God's Word is a revelation of His perfect will and it reflects His heart. Before looking up scripture, pray that God would help you understand the meaning and intention of the Word and help you to apply it to your life and circumstance. Don't pray what you want to have happen, but what God wants to have happen.

Let's say for example that you are concerned about safety in some situation that you are facing. You look up the word 'safe' in the Bible concordance or search word and are led to *Psalm 16:1-2, "Keep me safe, my God, for in you I take refuge. ² I say to the LORD, "YOU ARE MY LORD; APART FROM YOU I HAVE NO GOOD THING."* After reading this you may pray something like, "Lord, I know from your Word that when I take refuge in You, I am safe. Please keep me close to you and safe because I know that with You, I have only good things and without you I have no good things. In Jesus name, Amen." Beth Moore has a book called *Praying God's Word* which shows you how to turn scripture into prayers beautifully.

Nothing helps you identify with a scripture promise more than personalizing it. Putting your name right into the verse and speaking it out loud helps your heart to understand and believe that the promise is for YOU. Let's take one of my favorite verses; Jeremiah 29:11 and put your name in the verse. Mine would look like this:

> ¹¹ *For I know the plans I have for <u>Patty</u> declares the Lord, "plans to prosper <u>Patty</u> and not to harm <u>her</u>, plans to give <u>Patty</u> a hope and a future."*

Say that verse with your own name repeatedly and watch your heart start to believe it!

After you have found help in scripture and prayed it back to God, then seek Godly counsel from Christians that are in close relationship with God. Why is this important and how can you tell who would give you Godly council? *Matthew 7:16-18* sheds light on that issue:

> "$_{16}$ By their fruit you will recognize them. Do people pick grapes from thorn bushes, or figs from thistles? $_{17}$ Likewise, every good tree bears good fruit, but a bad tree bears bad fruit. $_{18}$ A good tree cannot bear bad fruit, and a bad tree cannot bear good fruit."

The verses above about fruit tell us that people's behavior reveals their hearts. A person who is close to God will bear good fruit. They will be trustworthy and true and live more like Jesus's example. You want to find people who know God enough to be able to tell you the truth about whether your direction would be inside the will of God or not. Remember, God's ways are higher than our ways. The advice from Godly council will line up with scripture and will be a safe decision for you to make.

Chances are that when all these things line up consistently, you are acting according to God's will and you can find peace in your decisions. While we can never be completely sure what God is up to, we can have a better idea of what He wants us to do if we use this practice consistently. Trust me, this practice has kept me out of trouble more than a few times!

Really P.R.A.Y.: The Skinny on Prayer Clip

Do you see yourself or someone you know in this humorous clip by the Skit Guys called the *Skinny on Prayer*?

The Skinny on Prayer

http://bit.ly/sSDlNW [24]

PattySadallah.com Other Books tab Paperback Film Links, Skinny on Prayer

I bet we give God a bit of a chuckle when He hears us praying like the silly parts of this clip. God just wants us to be real like Tommy at the end of the clip. He wants us to pray like we are having a conversation with Him. That is exactly what prayer is, a conversation with God. So why do most of us make it seem like a much bigger deal?

I don't know if our prayers frustrate, amuse or annoy God, but most of us approach prayer in the totally wrong way. Do you ever catch yourself praying for stuff that you think you "should" be praying for like the old joke about the beauty pageant contestant that talks about world peace just because she thinks it's expected?

Jesus called us His friends. For some of you it may be hard to grasp that Biblical truth. Jesus said *"I no longer call you servants, because a servant does not know his master's business. Instead, I have called you friends, for everything that I learned from my Father I have made known to you."~ John 15:15.* Would you go up to a friend and begin a conversation with: "Four score and seven years ago, our fathers brought forth to this continent, a new nation..."? How do you think your friend would respond to that conversation starter? It wasn't Abraham Lincoln's intention for people to simply memorize and recite the Gettysburg Address. He wanted them to truly understand the meaning of his words and his heart behind them.

It's interesting that just a few verses before the Lord's Prayer, Jesus warns us about insincere prayers when He says in *Matthew 6:5-8;* $_5$ *"And when you pray, do not be like the hypocrites, for they love to pray standing in the synagogues and on the street corners to be seen but I tell you, they have received their reward in full.* $_6$ *But when you pray, go into your room, close the door and pray to your Father, who sees what is done in secret, will reward you.* $_7$ *And when you pray, do not keep on babbling like pagans, for they think they will be heard because of their many words.* $_8$ *Do not be like them, for your Father knows what you need before you ask Him."* Let's not miss Jesus's point with this prayer.

Jesus showed us how to pray with the "Lord's Prayer". Wait a minute Patty, didn't you just say NOT to say prayers mindlessly and then you mention the one prayer people think of when you mention mindless prayers? Jesus was teaching us how to pray, not what to say when He prayed the Lord's Prayer with His disciples. The Lord's Prayer was intended to be a formula for prayer. We were supposed to grab the key elements of effective prayer, not the words themselves.

God wants us to be real with Him when we pray. He wants vulnerability and honesty. God wants us to pray Holy Spirit prayers: selfless, meaningful and honest prayers. He is not honored by prayers that are mindless repetitions of words.

> *Matthew 6:9-14, "This, then, is how you should pray: "'Our Father in heaven, hallowed be your name,$_{10}$ your kingdom come, your will be done, on earth as it is in heaven. $_{11}$ Give us today our daily bread. $_{12}$ And forgive us our debts, as we also have forgiven our debtors. $_{13}$ And lead us not into temptation,[a] but deliver us from the evil one.[b]' $_{14}$ For if you forgive other people when they sin against you, your Heavenly Father will also forgive you."*

When the Lord Jesus taught us to pray in Matthew, He was not teaching us to repeat the familiar words of the Lord's Prayer, He was giving us a model of prayer. He wanted us to P.R.A.Y. Let's look deeper at this prayer to see the key components that we can apply to our own prayer life.

Praise- Jesus began His prayer-model praising and honoring God. We should always begin our prayers by thanking God for all that He is and all that we are in Him. Thank Him for blessings, challenges, provisions, and family — anything for which you are grateful. If you have a hard time coming up with things for which to praise, sit quietly and journal until the page is full.

Repent – Confession is a key component in relationship with God. When you pray, ask God to search your heart for anything that offends Him. Have you noticed how many times forgive or forgiveness is mentioned in this prayer? The more we are honest with ourselves about areas that we need to forgive or confess, the closer we can become to God and the more He will hear our prayers. Ask God to give your heart a clean slate so that God can hear you and you can hear God. Forgiveness is the one component in this prayer example that is repeated. Without confession and forgiveness, we can't hear God and He won't hear our prayers.

Ask – God is not Santa or a Genie that we simply ask for what we want to happen. Then if it doesn't happen exactly the way we expect it to, we think that He wasn't listening or worse yet, that there mustn't be a God. People often think that God doesn't hear or answer their prayers because they are praying their own will. Remember, if it's not in your best interest, God will not answer yes. We should ask for God's perfect will.

Scripture reveals God's will in black and white. Take care to read the scriptures so you can learn about God's nature and His will in certain circumstances, then you can pray according to that truth. I believe that the Word of God is meant to be read as much as it is intended to be prayed back to God. So, pray the truth of scripture back to God and ask for His will to be done in your life. Regardless of the circumstances, we can trust that His way will be the right way.

We also need to have a healthy fear of the Evil one. What do I mean by a healthy fear? We need to acknowledge that there are forces fighting against us. Forgetting to pray for protection will keep us vulnerable to attacks from the enemy. *Ephesians 6:12, "For our struggle is not against flesh and blood, but against the rulers, against the authorities, against the powers of this dark world and against the spiritual forces of evil in the heavenly realms."*

It is also important to note that the Devil is not the opposite of God. He is a fallen angel. He can't hear your thoughts like God can. So to send him and his demons packing, you need to pray scripture out loud. Jesus is reminding us to keep on our guard every day for these negative influences and ask for protection.

Yield – Ask God for the courage and the willingness to do His will *this day*. Did you notice that Jesus didn't pray for tomorrow? He prayed for today. Pray that you can walk with Him today. That He will take care of your needs today and that you will please Him with your thoughts and actions today. God showed us through His provision of the manna for the wandering Israelites in the wilderness that His desire is for us to rely on Him one day at a time. If we are focused on the past, we will live with regrets. If we are looking too far in the future, we will live with the fear of the unknown. But if we trust God for THIS DAY, He will take care of us and walk with us through any and all challenges.

Then, end your prayers in the mighty and powerful name of Jesus Christ. When Jesus backs our prayers, there is power and authority. Here is an example of a prayer according to this model:

Heavenly Father,

(Praise) Thank you that you are my Provider, my Healer and my Comforter. Thank you that you are Sovereign and that Your will is perfect. Thank you for being as close as breathing and that I can count on you for any and all things. You are Sufficient. **(Repent)** Forgive me for any offensive thoughts or deeds that I have done today and bring to mind any un-forgiveness in my heart that needs to be cleansed (talk to God about specifics here). Clear my heart completely so that I can hear Your voice of guidance and direction. **(Ask)** Protect me from any evil schemes and prompt me to act according to Your will and make the steps and words clear for me today. Please take care of my physical body today. Heal me and restore me. I lift up ___ people and their needs. _____ **(Yield)** Help me to obey You in all things today. Order my day and remove any worry about finances or _____ that I may be carrying. Help me to trust you as my Sovereign God this day. In Jesus's Name, Amen.

Remember not to simply repeat the same prayer every day. But pray honestly each day including each of the elements of Praise, Repent, Ask and Yield.

Buh Bye Lymes and other Prayer Miracles

Getting Lymes disease was a gift. It slowed me down and brought me to a deeper level of relationship with my God. It was the beginning of a refiner's fire season that was absolutely necessary for me to grow in Christ enough to be able to fulfill my calling to write this book. Even though I got bitten by the Lymes tick in June of 2009, I didn't really get diagnosed until November of 2011 and didn't begin any sort of treatment regimen until January of 2012.

In early February of 2012, Mike Noble from Cleveland House of Prayer laid healing hands and prayed over me. He said that he felt the healing power of God shoot through His hands and into my body. He knew at that moment that I was healed.

But I expected it to look differently. So, I had lacked the faith to believe it at that time. When Lymes dies in a body it releases toxins and makes you sicker before you get better. This is called Herxing. I did feel a flush of Herx symptoms then and every time I was prayed over for my Lymes. But the everyday symptoms of Lymes not only remained but got stronger for more than a year after that initial prayer session. I knew that in God's heavenly timeline, I was already healed because God began the good work.

> *Philippians 1:6, "being confident of this, that He who began a good work in you will carry it on to completion until the day of Christ Jesus."*

I figured that God had some work to do in me before it would fully manifest in my body. I expected it to be a long process. Mike used to argue with me that God can evaporate toxins and that I didn't need to go through the Herxing pain if I believed in the healing. I think I frustrated Him for a year!

More than a year later, God spoke to me through the experience we were having with a Christian brother, Tim. Tim had been living with chronic pain from pancreatitis for 14 years. Tim's pancreas was producing stones that released painful enzymes into His body. The pancreas has more pain sensors than any organ and he was experiencing pain levels like that of a woman in labor for months.

Doctors could not solve this problem; so unfortunately, Tim was told that he would face a life sentence of mind-numbing pain killers if nothing could be done to take this pain away. He was only 28 years old. Tim and his wife Suzy were new friends of my daughter Jamael and my son-in-law, Nick. Jamael asked that we do a healing session at the Cleveland House of Prayer before

Tim would need to go to the hospital for a medical procedure; a temporary spinal blocking of pain, no long-term solution to the problem.

The night before that prayer session, God woke me up at 11:30 pm with an excitement and an anticipation that He was going to heal Tim. I was so excited to see how God would heal Tim that I could hardly get back to sleep. I learned later that God woke up Jamael and Suzy at about the same time that night and gave them the same assurance! With three people getting the same message from God, we knew that it was God's will to heal Tim.

Tim and his family came to the Cleveland House of Prayer and we had a heck of a prayer meeting. We prayed specific prayers that night; nothing vague or abstract. We prayed that God would knit Tim a new and healthy pancreas and that he would heal any residual damage that his poorly functioning organ had left in its wake. Miraculously, God dialed his pain down to a zero! Tim had not felt pain-free in years and he was pain free for 5 hours that night! But, just like I had been when Mike prayed for my healing, Tim was in a zombielike state of disbelief. He just couldn't wrap his head around it. Suzy believed that he was healed, but he did not. The next day, his pain returned, and he was discouraged. He went along with the procedure a few days later. It didn't work.

A second prayer session a week later was one of the coolest things that I have ever had the opportunity to experience. Tim walked into the prayer room with a pain level of a four (on a scale of 1-10) and he seemed readier to believe this time. His pain went down to about a one, but not all the way. Mike asked if we could sing in tongues for him. He said sure. My daughter

Jamael was watching Tim and Suzy's young daughters down the hallway and ran to see what sounded like 100 angels singing. Six of us were singing in tongues and it was like a chorus of Angels had joined us! Tim said that he literally felt God lift him off the ground like He was carrying him. He was profoundly moved by the experience. He left feeling surer that God had healed him this time.

Tim was able to rebuke the pain a few times himself afterward and understood it was more of a spiritual, rather than physical battle. But he started to lose his faith that God would take this pain away for good. He doubted that he was even worthy of God taking it completely away and was convincing himself that it was something he just needed to live with. He thought that he needed more coping skills. I felt like he was in spiritual quicksand. God wanted him to be pain free; the enemy wanted him in bondage to this pain and at the moment, he was agreeing with the enemy.

Tim reminds me of Peter. Peter was the first to say out loud that he believed that Jesus was the Messiah. He also denied Christ three times. Then after Jesus was resurrected, sitting around the campfire, Jesus asked Peter three times if he loved Him. Peter did love Jesus but needed to go deeper to really understand the kind of love that Jesus was talking about. Then, just a few short weeks after Jesus's ascension, Peter led thousands to Christ in a single speech. The name Peter means "the Rock of the Church" because Jesus knew that he would be a mighty man of God.

My friend Mary Elizabeth offered a prophetic word for Tim that she had received from God. Below are the notes that I took from it and shared with Tim.

> "Your struggle is with your identity. This pain and illness has been with you so long that it has become part of your identity. You struggle with the faith to believe because you are not sure how to be or live without it.
>
> You are wearing this illness like a heavy overcoat, all buttoned up, like a full body covering of you. But it is really a cloak, or a small caplet, loosely draped over your neck and shoulders. All you need to do is stand straight up, shrug your shoulders and walk forward toward God and it will fall right off. You will be free of it when you choose to be. God wants you to receive this new free identity. Choose to believe and let God free you of this past reality."

I shared this message with Tim, but he didn't quite understand it at first. He was still lost and still didn't believe that God really wanted him to be healed and pain free.

After sharing this incredible message with Tim and Suzy, I began to look at this message as helpful to anyone who is holding on to something as part of their identity that is a form of bondage. I prayed that God would show me what was hidden in my own heart that I needed to shrug my shoulders and let go of completely. At that moment, I felt a rush of Herxing symptoms. Interesting, I thought. Whatever it is that I need to face, it has something to do with the Lymes.

The next day I was in my Beth Moore *Breaking Free* Bible

class and God hit me over the side of the head. I knew that I was holding on to Lymes and I needed to let it go. It had become a kind of bondage to me. Later that day, Mary Elizabeth called me and gave me the exact same message. She told me that God wanted me to know that I can decide the day and time of my Lymes going away. God was ready to take it away, but I needed to lay it on the sacrificial altar and be ready to let it go. Two messages in the same day; I got you God! So, that night I prayed that God would reveal to me what it would take for me to let it go and for Him to take it away.

So, the next day I prayed and fasted and listened to worship music all day. I imagined myself writing a list of every Lymes symptom that I had ever experienced and listed each one on an imaginary paper: fuzzy headaches, earaches, loss of hearing, tinnitus, eczema, heart palpitations, pain in my lungs and kidneys, joint and muscle pain, nerve bundles in my feet, restless leg syndrome, and neuropathy. I imagined myself going to the cross and laying the sheet at the foot of the cross. I imagined Jesus hanging there above my head, dripping blood on me and on the papers. I was talking with Him and asking to not let me take them back. I had lots of real conversations with God in the Spirit that day.

I got sicker and sicker as the day went on. I napped wearing earphones and kept waking to songs about God wanting me to be free and God as Healer, etc. By evening, I had a splitting migraine and needed to go to bed. I awoke at 8:26pm and threw up a very large quantity of liquid which was odd because I hadn't really had anything to eat and not much to drink all day. I went back to bed.

At 9:26pm, I had another round of vomiting and the strangest thing happened. It was what I imagine being beamed aboard the Star Trek Enterprise would feel like — static electric feeling under my skin on my arms and legs that lasted maybe 15 seconds. Then it felt like God had an eraser and swipe, swipe, swiped the feeling away. Like it was on a white board and He erased it. I said out loud "God you took it away!" And I praised God for it and fell back asleep.

At 10:26pm I woke, vomited and when I got back to bed, I had the exact same experience; this time it was in my torso. I could feel it in my chest and belly and all over my back. It was the same electrical feeling and the same eraser swiping. It was so cool! I was praising God even more.

I woke up again at 11:26pm and had my fourth and final episode. I felt the same odd feeling in my neck and up to my pounding head, then the slightest feelings of it being swiped away like the other two times. I started to cry and said to God, "And from my lips you drew the *Hallelujah*." It was a line from one of my favorite songs; Jason Castro's Hallelujah. And God gave me Glory Bumps.

I woke up one more time about 3 hours later. This time, I was completely pain free; no headaches or body aches. It was finished. I praised and thanked God even more. God is so cool! What an amazing assurance that He has given me.

When I woke up in the morning, I knew that the Lymes was gone. It served a purpose for a season, but God didn't want it to become part of my identity and He allowed me to leave it at the foot of the cross. God gave me the glimpse of the pain-free completed healing. God is faithful and always finishes what He starts! Amen to the King of Kings!

What was with the 26? I knew that it wasn't a coincidence, so I looked up verses in the Bible with 26 and God led me to *Matthew 19:26 "'Jesus looked at them and said, "With man this is impossible, but with God all things are possible."'* Amen!

What happened to Tim?

Tim was really struggling for about a month after his healing miracle and was in a real funk. His pain was back with a vengeance and his wife Suzy, Jamael and I decided that he needed a Jesus encounter. So we prayed that God would show up in his dreams and give him a 'road to Damascus' experience like the Apostle Paul's encounter that would increase his faith. We really believed that if he could see and feel the love of Jesus up close and personal, it would change his life. We didn't want to tell God how to go about that, but we wanted God to show Tim how much He loved him, and that God really did want him completely healed.

Tim had to go back into the hospital because his pain level was out of control and his pain medicine was gone. So, he spent a week in the hospital just on medication to cope with the pain. It wasn't until the night that he got home from the hospital that he told Suzy about the dreams. He didn't even want to share the dreams because they were so horrifying.

The dreams happened over several days and they were the most terrifying thing that Tim has ever experienced. There were some where Tim was getting beat up, some where he was shot, or knifed. They were horrible battle dreams and he kept getting back up. "These were not like dreams, they were realer than real." Tim said.

In one of his dreams, the battle killed Tim and he wound up at the gates of heaven. There he encountered Jesus and was given a glimpse. God told him that He was a man of his Word and because Tim had accepted Christ as his Lord and Savior, he was welcome, but that he had failed him. God had much bigger plans for him and he did not rise up and serve God fully. God showed him that heaven has floors, the lowest levels are for those who accepted Christ but did very little to love people or advance the kingdom, the higher the level, the more rewards people had earned and the closer they were to God. Tim would spend eternity on one of the lower levels. He was still standing at the gate, but God allowed him to peak through. Tim fell to his knees in regret for not having done more for God.

Next God showed him how things would work out for his wife and children. They would grieve, but eventually move on to serve God well. Then, God showed Tim how his life can be if he chose to live for God. Tim saw himself completely healthy and his family totally happy together. He was serving God with joy. He knew without any question that it was God's will for him to be healthy and happy.

When Suzy heard these dreams, she was jumping around for joy. Tim was confused by this reaction. She shared that this was a direct answer to prayer and explained to Tim that God loved him so much that He wanted to make it abundantly clear that He wanted him healed and pain free. God could have taken him for real and he could actually be in heaven regretting his choices, but God gave him this chance to make it right. What a loving and merciful God we serve! Tim had been looking at these dreams like a death sentence, but they were sent to give him hope.

A short time later, Tim learned that the pain that he was still feeling was not from his pancreas, it was from his pain medication. The cycle of needing the meds and then taking them and having them wear off, was causing him pain.

Tim knew that God wanted him whole and healed. He admitted himself into a rehab for the pain medication addiction and is now drug free. God birthed a calling in his heart to help people who are in bondage to drugs and other addictions. He is free!

Praise God that Tim is still feeling great and has been able to be more attentive to his family. Tim recalled "One of the biggest things I learned from the whole ordeal was that I was depending on the medication to handle my pain. I realized that the medication was separating me from my relationship with Christ." That can be true of anything we try to make our savior: only Jesus can be our Savior.

Tim said, "Before I had a shaky foundation but now God is allowing me to build a strong foundation in Him one brick at a time." He is seeking God for His will and is regaining his strength. God is now more able to bless Tim because he is no longer fighting with God. God is planting seeds and preparing him for service in the future. He has found victory over other strongholds as well. God is really blessing his family!

Tim's wife Suzy is a gifted poetic writer and she sent me a prayer that I think sums up how it feels to be living beyond bondage. Here it is:

"Lord God, today I celebrate progress.

Like Abraham walking down Mount Sinai with Isaac alongside Him;

like Job surrounded by new prosperity and blessings;

like Joshua standing amidst the rubble of a freshly fallen Jericho;

like Joseph in his royal garments as he embraced his brothers;

like Mary when she saw the risen Christ and touched the wounds of His hands...

I will celebrate my progress today, having defeated death by the grace of God, I stand on the Rock of Salvation and take in all that the Lord that has done for me."

~ Suzy Beinecke

The moral of these stories is that God stands waiting for us to ask Him through prayer for big miracles. He wants only the best for us. We just need to have the boldness to ask and be ready to receive His blessings when they come. This is not magic; it is the power of the Holy Spirit!

After Jesus ascended to heaven and the Holy Spirit was given to them, the apostles were able to perform miracles as great as Jesus did.

Acts 5:12-16, "The apostles performed many signs and wonders among the people. And all the believers used to meet together in Solomon's Colonnade. $_{13}$ No one else dared join them, even though they were highly regarded by the people. $_{14}$ Nevertheless, more and more men and women believed in the Lord and were added to their number. $_{15}$ As a result, people brought the sick into the streets and laid them on beds and mats so that at least Peter's shadow might fall on some of them as he passed by. $_{16}$ Crowds gathered also from the towns around Jerusalem, bringing their sick and those tormented by impure spirits, and all of them were healed."

Did you catch that even Peter's shadow had healing power? Let me ask you something; is the Holy Spirit in Peter different than the one in me or you if you are a believer? Nope. It's the same exact Holy Spirit. All believers who have faith can pray for anything that is in God's will and God will answer those prayers, even if they seem impossible to man. The closer you get to God the more you will align your head and heart, the more you will pray according to God's will, and the more prayers and miracles you will see in your life.

Life Application: NORTH

1. Reflect on what it means that the Bible is one long love story. How does that make you look at the Bible differently?

2. Let's practice that exercise mentioned in the book: pick up your Bible, close your eyes, and pray that God would lead you to the exact verse that He wants you to have for today. Journal here what verse God led you to and what you think He's trying to communicate to you about that verse. How does it relate to your life today?

3. Understanding who God is and who you are as a child of the living God is so critical to living the abundant Christian life. What truth about God or about you do you have the most trouble believing? Ask God to increase your faith in those areas in a prayer here.

4. In retrospect, has God ever answered the prayer completely differently than you expected like what happened in the video with Capt. Dan?

5. Let's practice looking up Scripture that you may need to solve a problem. Go to your Bible concordance or Bible Gateway at www.BibleGateway.com and practice searching a word related to a challenge or issue that you may be facing right now. What did you learn about your issue from the Bible by searching the verses? Take one Scripture verse and look it up in a different version if you are on Bible Gateway or have another version of the Bible handy. How did each version give you a different perspective on the same verse?

6. Choose any of the verses that you've already found, and practice creating a prayer using that verse.

7. Using the P. R. A. Y. Model, write your own prayer for today.

8. Since it's the same Holy Spirit that lives in you that lived in the Apostles, what miracle can you pray for and ask the Holy Spirit's power to make it happen? Remember, prayers that are according to God's sovereign will always answer yes.

WEST
Overcoming Life's Challenges and Finding Forgiveness

When I saw that God had included this section in the model for me to write about, I had a sinking feeling that I was headed for learning some painful lessons during the process of writing. God brought back lots of memories of heroes of the faith that I have had the pleasure to know and some past hurts which I needed to let go. That process blessed me and brought me a lot of healing. God also introduced me to some other amazingly victorious people since the original assignment to write this book so that I can share their stories with you also. It provided a multitude of blessings!

Life is going to be tough. That's a promise. It's really what you do with it that counts. Marcia Lange passed that test with flying colors. Marcia was a volunteer in my department when I worked at the Parmadale Training Institute. Marcia was an insulin-dependent Type 1 diabetic since the age of six and unfortunately followed in her family's footsteps by becoming an alcoholic from a very early age. Alcohol and diabetes make a very dangerous combination.

Marcia and I had many conversations about God, and we grew very close. I will never forget the story of her salvation. Marcia had been drinking heavily that night and went into a diabetic coma that killed her. She was dead for about 8 minutes before the paramedics were able to revive her. During that time, she had a visit to hell.

Marcia had always resisted organized religion and was angry at God for making her diabetic and for her dysfunctional family and social life that kept her perpetually overwhelmed and angry. She described hell as a dark, cold and lonely place where she was haunted by her regrets. She never saw the light and she never saw God, but she recalled God speaking to her and asking her if this was the eternal destination she desired. She was overcome with shame and regret and promised that if she were able to get a second chance, she would turn her life around.

The paddles jolted Marcia back to life and she had that chance. She asked Christ into her heart as soon as she was conscious. Even though her health issues had her on disability by the time she was in her early thirties, Marcia kept her promise to God and turned her life around. She served the Lord in volunteer positions with joy and humility.

Marcia died for the second time a few years later. This was also temporary. This time she was able to get a glimpse of heaven and had a face-to-face conversation with God. She recalled the immeasurable love she felt from God and the beauty and peace of heaven. It was a very different experience from her first death. She didn't want to leave heaven, but once again she was returned back to her even more feeble body. She was not sure why God brought her back that time, but she never had a fear of death after that visit to heaven.

Marcia's life got a lot tougher after her second resurrection. I remember her saying; "One day you will hear that I am dead, for good this time, and when that happens, I want you to promise me that you will dance a jig on my grave." She knew that in death she would be more alive with no pain and suffering for eternity. That truth was jig worthy!

Marcia's health deteriorated and she was no longer able to volunteer. I also left that job, but Marcia and I kept in touch from time to time. I visited her in the hospital after her leg amputation, caused by diabetes. She had so much joy that day lying on the hospital bed. She wasn't bitter. She wasn't angry. She had Jesus and that was enough. Marcia had learned to live with an eternal perspective. She was content regardless of her circumstances because she was focused on the next life.

I learned an important lesson from Marcia about the value of having an eternal perspective. I remember her saying without a hint of sarcasm that day, "God must really love me!" It struck me as such an odd comment considering her circumstance, so I asked her what she meant by it. She said, "God must love me to give me so much challenge and pain in my life and to rescue me from certain hell. Because I will earn a crown of life and have some pretty sweet accommodations in heaven! And since heaven is forever, I think I will have made out big time in the end!" *James 1:12, "Blessed is the one who perseveres under trial because, having stood the test, that person will receive the **crown of life** that the Lord has promised to those who love Him."* The crown of life is one of the special rewards earned by those who persevere under trials.

One of the biggest regrets in my life was the day that I felt the Holy Spirit prompt me to call Marcia and I didn't do it. It was before cell phones and I was in the car when I got the prompting. When I got home and busy, I completely forgot to call her. It was a few days later I got the call from Marcia's sister saying she died. Her sister said that Marcia wanted to say goodbye to me the day that I was prompted to call her because she knew she was dying. Her sister only knew my first name and it took a while for her to find my number. It brings tears to my eyes at this moment as I remember the sadness that I felt for missing that opportunity. Even though I felt silly, I kept my promise to dance a jig on her grave and I felt her laughing with joy in heaven.

Marcia learned the lesson that all of us need to learn. This life is a snap of your finger compared to eternity. We all have lessons to learn from our trials and, if we pass those tests and learn to lean on Jesus and represent Him well, we will have eternal rewards 100-fold better than anything we endured in this short life. Here is proof of that truth from the scriptures: *Zephaniah 3:19-20,*

> *"[19] At that time I will deal*
>
> *with all who oppressed you.*
>
> *I will rescue the lame;*
>
> *I will gather the exiles.*
>
> *I will give them praise and honor*

> *in every land where they have suffered shame.*
>
> [20] *At that time I will gather you;*
>
> *at that time I will bring you home.*
>
> *I will give you honor and praise*
>
> *among all the peoples of the earth*
>
> *when I restore your fortunes*[a]
>
> *before your very eyes,"*
>
> *says the* LORD."

Jesus promised that we will be repaid for all of our sacrifices 100-fold in these verses from *Mark 10,* " [29] *"Truly I tell you," Jesus replied, "no one who has left home or brothers or sisters or mother or father or children or fields for me and the gospel* [30] *will fail to receive a hundred times as much in this present age: homes, brothers, sisters, mothers, children and fields—along with persecutions—and in the age to come eternal life.* [31] *But many who are first will be last, and the last first."'*

Marcia knew that the time we spend on this earth is like a single grain of sand on all of the beaches on earth compared to forever in eternity. So, whatever you endure on earth will be quickly forgotten in heaven if you accept Jesus's free gift. You too can have some eternally "sweet accommodations!"

It's not a dead end . . . Clip 1 from Unconditional

Tissue alert for these next two clips from the movie *Unconditional.* This movie trailer does a wonderful job of telling the back story of this amazing film based on true events in the life of Joe Bradford. (The events related to Sam and Billy Crawford in this film are fictional.)

Unconditional 1

http://www.bit.ly/TObVhb [25]

PattySadallah.com Other Books tab Paperback Film Links, Unconditional 1

Before watching the second clip, I wanted to share some more of the film story. Joe Bradford found Jesus in prison after spending some time in solitary confinement. After his release, Joe moved back to the projects on a mission to help the fatherless children in inner city Nashville, TN. He became known as Papa Joe to the kids; caring for them as a loving father figure. When his childhood best friend Sam and he reconnected,

Joe was dying of kidney failure and Sam was grieving over the murder of her husband Billy.

Sam's husband Billy was a Godly man who showed the love of Christ by reaching out to strangers with love and $2 bills. The bills were his symbol of love. Sam explained that there are millions of them in print, but they are hardly ever seen. People hide them away or hoard them. Billy's philosophy was that "there was enough love to go around, you just got to share it." Along with random acts of kindness, Billy passed the $2 bills on to people everywhere he went.

Sam was overcome with grief and obsessed about finding her husband's killer and exacting her revenge. She thought she knew who her husband's killer was; Anthony, a man from Papa Joe's neighborhood. Sam was prepared to kill him when she learned the truth about her husband's death from Anthony. Billy had reached out to Anthony that fateful rainy night and shared the love of Christ. When Billy's car wouldn't start, Anthony fixed it for him. When Anthony walked away and turned the corner, he heard a shot and ran back to Billy. Billy knew that he would not survive, so he handed Anthony a picture Sam had drawn of the Firebird with a $2 bill on the back and told him to promise to tell her to finish the book and always walk on the clouds. Then Billy died in Anthony's arms. Anthony knew that he would be suspected of the killing, so he ran. But he was never the same. That conversation changed his heart and his life.

No Storm Can Take the Son Away – Clip 2 from Unconditional

Unconditional 2

http://bit.ly/19yU2Ls [26]

PattySadallah.com Other Books tab Paperback Film Links, Unconditional 2

The children's book referenced in the clip, *The Firebird*[27] holds the key message of this film. Sam writes of a small Oriel bird named Firebird who asks her mother why God gives storms the power to take the sun away. The mother bird tells the little bird that someday, when you take a walk on the clouds, you will see for yourself and learn the truth about the sun.

When the bird was just learning how to fly there was a mighty storm and his mother encouraged him to see for himself. He flew higher and higher with lightening, thunder and howling winds and he thought that the storm would break him apart. Just when he was about to lose all strength, he broke through the clouds and there it was. The sun was shining more beautiful than ever. At that moment it became clear that no storm can take the sun away. The sun is always shining. It was as constant as his mother's love. You just need to take a walk on the clouds.

No one can take the Son away. Jesus talks about this in *John 10:29*, *"My Father, who has given them to me, is greater than all; no one can snatch them out of my Father's hand."* And God's promise is affirmed in *1 Corinthians 10:13*, *"No temptation has overtaken you except what is common to mankind. And God is faithful; He will not let you be tempted beyond what you can bear. But when you are tempted, He will also provide a way out so that you can endure it."*

God allows challenges in our lives for a reason. It may take a lifetime for us to understand what He was up to when we go through the trials of life. We may not even understand until we get to heaven. I love what Papa Joe said about that, "It's not a dead end if it takes you somewhere you needed to go." The secret is to learn the lessons in each and every trial of life by leaning on and trusting God to get you through them. Only then can you continue to grow and help others.

Papa Joe Bradford survived his kidney transplant and is still serving kids in Nashville and around the country with his wife Denise. Thousands of kids have been loved and mentored by them through their ministry, Elijah's Heart. The children in this film were all from Papa Joe's program; they were not professional actors. Learn more about them and their amazing ministry at www.PapaJoe.org. [28]

Slingshot Faith

It's amazing what a person can handle with the strength of Jesus. *Philippians 4:13 (NLT)*, *"For I can do everything through*

Christ,[a] who gives me strength." God brought Sam to the point where she knew forgiveness was the only way to set herself free from the bondages of her past.

*1 Peter 5:2-4 (MSG) "Be shepherds of God's flock that is under your care, watching over them—not because you must, but because you are willing, as God wants you to be; not pursuing dishonest gain, but eager to serve; not lording it over those entrusted to you, but being examples to the flock. And when the Chief Shepherd appears, you will receive the **crown of glory** that will never fade away."*

We can't control what happens to us in this life. But we absolutely can control how we react to it.

Kevin Baldwin calls that kind of power from Christ slingshot faith. Kevin, who was formerly homeless, is a life coach who learned the same lesson. Having found victory over a poverty mentality and a violent childhood, Kevin shared the slingshot metaphor with me one day. He said that just as the slingshot can throw a stone farther the more it is stretched backwards, the more impact a believer has when they can find victory over life's challenges. In other words, if you have never had a challenge, or a trial or a painful situation, then how can you possibly help someone who has? Our life challenges are all meant to teach us something and they are meant to be used to help other people.

This lifetime is a snap of your fingers; eternity is forever. What will you do with your life challenges?

Getting to Forgiveness: Clip from October Baby

We all have legitimate reasons to be angry. The truth is, you can't get through life without people hurting you. In the film *October*

Baby, Hannah learns that she is adopted and that her lifelong health issues are caused by her premature birth due to a failed abortion.

October Baby

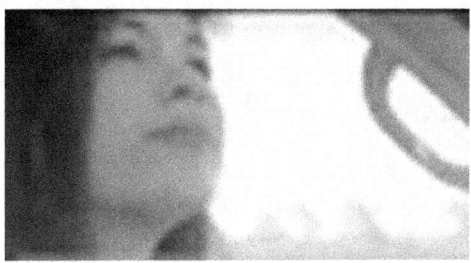

http://bit.ly/1hKQ9UI [29]

See PattySadallah.com Other Books tab Paperback Film Links, October Baby

In an earlier scene in the movie, Hannah visited her biological mother at her office. The woman was stunned to see her. At first, the birth mother seemed like she was interested in talking, until her husband walked into the office to take her to lunch. She got flustered and when her husband asked who Hannah was, she answered "nobody" and told her that she had to go. The heartbreak from this second rejection was palpable.

Hannah had gone on a trip to make sense of this new truth that she was a survivor of a failed abortion, and that her twin brother had died shortly after her parents adopted them. Can you relate to Hannah's anger toward her parents for keeping that secret from her? Or how about the pain of knowing that your birth mother really didn't want you?

The priest in the clip refers to *Colossians 3:13*. Here it is in the Amplified Bible (AMP) version: *"Be gentle and forbearing with one another and, if one has a difference (a grievance or complaint) against another, readily pardoning each other; even as the Lord has [freely] forgiven you, so must you also [forgive]."* There were so many wonderful Biblical nuggets in that chapel scene. There were four words that the priest said that were critical in that scene: power, choice, burden and free.

He said that because we have been forgiven by God, we have the *power* to forgive others. The Holy Spirit gives us the power to forgive. It's not something we can do of our own strength. So many times, we try to let things go on our own, but there is a nagging voice in our heads that keeps us from forgetting the hurts and we just can't let it go. It is only when we pray to God to take it away that the Holy Spirit does a work in our hearts to let our hurts go.

I love how the priest talked about anger and resentment as a *"burden* you no longer need to carry." A burden is something that weighs us down. It's a heavy load, an emotional stress that oppresses us; like carrying this massive thing around all the time. It's exhausting. Forgiveness is a *choice*. You have to decide in your heart that you are ready to forgive. God won't do it for you without your cooperation. You have to choose to let hurts go. You can choose to drop off that burden. When you do, God is ready to take it from you.

The priest in the clip quoted *John 8:36 "So if the Son sets you free, you will be free indeed."* Do you know what it's like to be released from something? I mean really released from it where that memory or place or person can't hurt you anymore. You still remember, but you don't have the pain from the memory anymore. It is a feeling that I have only known with the power of the Holy Spirit. When Hannah gave that note to her biological mother, it was finished. She didn't know or even need to know what her biological mom's reaction was. God healed her the moment the note was left on the desk. I love the smile on her face at the end of that clip. You can see the release of her burden on her face.

October Baby was not based on an actual true story. It was intended to speak the phenomenon of survivors of abortion and forgiveness. But, in the special features of the DVD, Shari Rigby, the actress that played Hannah's birth mother, shared that her life had paralleled the character she was portraying. She too was a young professional working in a law firm when she became pregnant. She had an abortion and had always regretted her decision. Shari shared that when they filmed the scene depicted in this clip, she was not acting. We were witnessing her real emotional release of the pain of her own decision so many years ago. She shared that she and God did a mighty work together in filming day and she really was released from her own personal burden. God is good!

Dad's Transformation Clip from Undaunted: The Early Life of Josh McDowell

We have already touched on Josh McDowell's story of his journey to Christ and a bit of his impact since his salvation day earlier in the book. In this clip from *Undaunted: The Early Life of Josh McDowell,* Josh tells the incredible story of his father's salvation and subsequent impact.

Undaunted

http://bit.ly/1cHs9E4 [30]

See PattySadallah.com Other Books tab Paperback Film Links, Undaunted

For most of his life, Wilmot McDowell, Sr. was an abusive alcoholic. He often beat his wife and children and was one of the reasons for Josh's hard heart toward God when he was young. Earlier scenes in the movie reveal that he was so disrespected that his oldest son was able to get a court order to take the house off its foundation and move it from his father's possession.

Josh decided that he needed to forgive his father. He needed to free himself from anger and hatred for his dad that held him hostage. So, one day he met his father at the coffee shop and told him that he loved him, that he forgave him and that God loved him. Dad was stunned and had no reply at the time. Josh didn't do it for his dad; he did it for himself. He did it because God's Word says in *Matthew 6:15, "But if you do not forgive others their sins, your Father will not forgive your sins."* Josh didn't do it with his own strength either. He did it through the power of the Holy Spirit.

Josh prayed for his father but didn't expect his father to change. When his father asked Jesus into his life, it was an answer to prayer. Fourteen months later, Wilmot died of complications of his long-term abuse of alcohol. A decision for Christ does not exempt you from the consequences of your sin.

"Scores" of people came to Christ because he shared his testimony with them. A score is 20, and that was a plural word. Think about that reality considering that his father only lived 14 months from the day of his salvation. No one would have predicted that the last 14 months of Wilmot McDowell's life would be so fruitful.

Most of us can be believers for 30 or 40 years and not have that kind of Kingdom impact. Wilmot's story is a testament that as long as you draw breath, it's not too late to turn your life around and change your eternal residence. There is nothing as contagious as a life completely transformed by the power of the Holy Spirit!

How to Set the Captive Free

Right about now, I bet you are asking, "Patty, it's great that all these people have been able to overcome challenges and find forgiveness, but *how* do *I* do that?" I prayed about this for a long time. I wanted to tell you a true story of how I was able to overcome past hurt and find forgiveness. God gave me the idea to tell my story and allow you to tell your own at the same time. This may seem a little weird, but as you read this story circle the parts or fill in others that relate to your life. I challenge you to follow your own story to its victorious conclusion. I pray that God will use this opportunity to show you the way to find the forgiveness you need in your own life.

Fill in the blanks with the name or pronoun that makes sense for you.

There was this (man/ woman/ couple) that (disappointed/ hurt/ abused/ neglected) me (once/ consistently/ repeatedly over time). This (memory/ behavior) seemed to have a cumulative effect on me. Each (offense/ memory of the offense) would reinforce my pain. It would re-open a raw wound in me. I (resented/ disliked/ hated) (_____) and just couldn't let it go.

I prayed to God over and over for Him to make (_____) change. But to no avail. This offensive behavior was so consistent that I began to wonder why I ever expected a different behavior. This was their's normal behavior. This season of time (is still happening/ lasted _____ period of time).

Then one day, I prayed a new prayer.

I wanted to understand (_____). So I prayed that God would help me to see things from their perspective. I wanted to know what made them behave like the way they did. I also prayed that God would help me see (_____) from His eyes.

That prayer changed everything.

God showed me a glimpse of the future consequences that (_____) (behavior/ decisions/ attitudes) will have on their future. I was able to see (_____) many years into the future and I saw a (sad/ lonely/ isolated/ sick) (person/ couple) that was living out the consequences of the decisions of their past. I suddenly felt a compassion for them that I didn't know was there.

I felt my own heart shift from less anger and more compassion and love for them. I felt sorry for them; sorry for what (_____) (was/ were) missing in life and sorry that (_____) would wind up living or dying and suffering the full measure of consequences for their behavior.

This glimpse softened my heart and caused me to pray new prayers for them.

I started to pray blessings instead of curses for him/ her. I prayed for healing, salvation, a strong relationship with God, forgiveness, prosperity, reconciliation, restored loving relationships, freedom from strongholds, and fruitful impact.

I noticed a change in me first. The mention of (_____) name(s) that once made me recoil now prompted me to say a quick prayer for them. The oddest thing happened next. I noticed a change in (him/ her/ them). I hadn't really expected new behavior from (_____) so this change was a surprise. It wasn't an earth-shattering change, but something was there; something softer. There was (more respect/ more responsibility/ more consideration/ less hostility/ less inappropriate behavior/ _____). I also began to see a positive change in our relationship.

God changed us. And it started with a new prayer.

My story is still a work in progress, and I wish that I could say that things are perfect, but no one is perfect. When God softens a hard heart, He performs a miracle of release that frees the captive, the person that needs to be forgiven and hopefully you. You may not live to see a change in the person that offended you. And in fact, that person may not even still be alive, but God will work healing in your own heart if you ask Him to.

Let's summarize what it takes to set the captive free: First we need to ask God to give us a new prayer. Prayer is the mechanism for the Holy Spirit to do His thing. If you want someone to change, you need to change first. Ask God to help you understand the situation or circumstance and what you are supposed to learn from it. Ask God to show you the new prayer that will work to resolve this situation. Praying blessings instead of curses is the key to resolution. Pray as though God has already solved the problem.

This is not the only way or the only prayer that will move you toward forgiveness. Ask God to show you the right prayer for your circumstance.

Paul prayed a fantastic prayer in *Ephesians 3:14 "For this reason I kneel before the Father, [15] from whom every family[a] in heaven and on earth derives its name. [16] I pray that out of His glorious riches He may strengthen you with power through His Spirit in your inner being, [17] so that Christ may dwell in your hearts through faith. And I pray that you, being rooted and established in love, [18] may have power, together with all the Lord's holy people, to grasp how wide and long and high and deep is the love of Christ, [19] and to know this love that surpasses knowledge—that you may be filled to the measure of all the fullness of God. [20] Now to Him who is able to do immeasurably more than all we ask or imagine, according to His power that is at work within us, [21] to Him be glory in the church and in Christ Jesus throughout all generations, forever and ever! Amen."*

Pray that kind of prayer for the person that came to mind with the story and see what happens! Don't expect them to change. God wants this to be about you and Him first and foremost. Expect a greater feeling of peace about the situation in your own heart. God may very well change them too, like in my story. That will be a double blessing.

What if the one you need to forgive is you?

We are all sinners. Not one person other than Jesus Himself has gotten through this life without sin. *Romans 3:23, "For everyone has sinned; we all fall short of God's glorious standard."* That's the very reason that it was necessary for Jesus to come and die for us in the first place!

The first step is to agree with God that you have sinned. This is called confession and it is the key to unlocking God's mercy. *Proverbs 28:13, "People who conceal their sins will not prosper, but if they confess and turn from them, they will receive mercy."* If there is something in your life that you know is hurting others or yourself, you can find freedom from it just like Wilmot McDowell and the actress playing the birth mother in October Baby did.

What happens when we confess our sins to God? *1 John 1:7-9, "But if we are living in the light, as God is in the light, then we have fellowship with each other, and the blood of Jesus, His Son, cleanses us from all sin. If we claim we have no sin, we are only fooling ourselves and not living in the truth. But if we confess our sins to Him, He is faithful and just to forgive us our sins and to cleanse us from all wickedness."*

God knows everything about you and He still loves you. His heart's desire is to free you from your bondages and from the sins that entangle. He promises victory over sin in *1 Corinthians 15:57* says, *"But thank God! He gives us victory over sin and death through our Lord Jesus Christ."* Romans 8:1, *"So now there is no condemnation for those who belong to Christ Jesus."* God doesn't expect us to be perfect. That's why Jesus came to Earth in the first place. Whatever you have done, God is ready to forgive you.

The secret to forgiving yourself is the same secret as what it takes to forgive others. Pray a new prayer. *2 Corinthians 5:17, "Therefore if any man be in Christ, he is a new creature: old things are passed away; behold, all things are become new."* If you have asked God to forgive you for your sins over and over and still feel guilty, you don't believe God's promises are true. Don't let Satan trick you into believing that lie. Failing to believe God for who He says He is, and who He says you are, is a fast track to bondage. *Micah 7:19 says "You will again have compassion on us; you will tread our sins underfoot and hurl all our iniquities into the depths of the sea."* God has said it. You need to believe it. The new prayer that you may need to pray is one that will increase your faith to believe that God has forgiven you. Ask God to show you how He sees you. Ask God to release you from your guilt and shame. Pray for the Holy Spirit to give you the power to stay on track. God is faithful.

If you have offended someone, God wants you to make it right. Jesus welcomed Zacchaeus, the Chief Tax Collector, to repent of his sin of overcharging the citizens and lining his own pockets. Let's see what his response was after being convicted in his heart: *Luke 19:8, "But Zacchaeus stood up and said to the Lord, 'Look, Lord! Here and now I give half of my possessions to the poor, and if I have cheated anybody out of anything, I will pay back four times the amount.'"*

What was Jesus' reaction to his repentance?

> *[9] Jesus said to him, "Today salvation has come to this house, because this man, too, is a son of Abraham. [10] For the Son of Man came to seek and to save the lost."*

Zacchaeus agreed with Jesus that overcharging was a sin and he made a commitment to make it right. He found forgiveness. Jesus, the Son of Man, came for people like Zacchaeus and for me and you. God will show you what He wants you to do if you need to ask someone for forgiveness. Remember, you won't have to do it of your own power. The Holy Spirit will come along side you and the captive that will be set free is you.

What if the one you need to forgive is God?

Are you mad at God? Losing a child or a parent to a drunk driver or a murderer is hard to understand. Maybe you are living with sickness or are mad that God created you with disabilities. Maybe you are mad that God hasn't answered your prayers for healing. God doesn't want tragic things to happen to us, but He does allow them. God is Sovereign. *Romans 8:28, "And we know that **in all things** God works for the good of those who love Him, who have been called according to His purpose."*

There is always a lesson in every life trial or challenge. Marcia learned that no matter what you must endure in life; God has a blessing in it for you. God has your best in mind even if it seems like your life is out of control.

It's all about changing your prayers. When you are mad at God, it's important to go to the Word and see what God has promised for you.

"Can anything ever separate us from Christ's love? Does it mean He no longer loves us if we have calamity, or are persecuted, or hungry, or destitute, or in danger or threatened with death? No! Despite all these things, overwhelming victory is ours through Christ who loved us." Romans 8:35-37. If you have accepted Christ as your Savior, God is tethered to you. He will always be there.

"The Lord is close to the brokenhearted. He rescues those whose spirits are crushed." Psalm 34:18 (New Living Translation) God knows you are hurting and wants to comfort you.

And we know God causes everything to work together for the good of those who love God and are called according to His purpose for them." Romans 8:28 (NLT) God can turn around ANYTHING for good.

Cling on to those promises. Ask Him to show you what you are supposed to learn. Praise Him regardless of your circumstances.

I'll never forget the funeral I attended for Jeff, a 12-year-old classmate of my daughter. Even though this child was a great swimmer, he had a heart attack at the community pool and tragically died. His aunt died the same way at the same age and it was learned that there was a hereditary heart condition. Jeff's death raised the awareness of the condition in the family and he may have saved a sibling's life.

When I walked into the funeral the first thing that I noticed was Jeff's mom, Theresa, comforting Jeff's best friend. She was praying with him and encouraging him. I was so amazed by her loving response.

Most people would be so mad at God for taking their first-born son. And Jeff's parents may have had some of those feelings, but by the time I saw them, they had enough comfort from the Holy Spirit that they were able to share it with others. A ministry was born out of their tragedy and now they lead a ministry comforting families in times of grief.

God wants you to need Him and let Him take care of things for you. Let Him. There is a blessing around the corner in every difficult and challenging circumstance if you look for it. God has already seen the whole picture. He knows every turn your life will take. He knew that breaking up with Fred would lead me to a better place long before Fred and I ever met. Remember, it's not a dead end if it takes you somewhere you need to go. So, when life throws you a major curve ball, trust that God does have your best interest in mind and lean into His capable arms.

> *Romans 8:31-39 (MSG) "So, what do you think? With God on our side like this, how can we lose? If God didn't hesitate to put everything on the line for us, embracing our condition and exposing Himself to the worst by sending His own Son, is there anything else He wouldn't gladly and freely do for us? And who would dare tangle with God by messing with one of God's chosen? Who would dare even to point a finger? The One who died for us—who was raised to life for us!—is in the presence of God at this very moment sticking up for us. Do you think anyone is going to be able to drive a wedge between us and Christ's love for us? There is no way! Not trouble, not hard times, not hatred, not hunger, not homelessness, not bullying threats, not backstabbing, not even the worst sins listed in Scripture:*
>
> *They kill us in cold blood because they hate you.*
>
> *We're sitting ducks; they pick us off one by one.*
>
> *None of this fazes us because Jesus loves us. I'm absolutely convinced that nothing—nothing living or dead, angelic or demonic, today or tomorrow, high*

or low, thinkable or unthinkable—absolutely nothing can get between us and God's love because of the way that Jesus our Master has embraced us."

God loves you and wants your best. He allows difficult and unpleasant challenges to come into our lives so that we may learn to let Him show us the way to freedom and blessings. Sometimes He uses the worst experiences in our lives to bring us a special calling so we can help others. Marcia focused on heaven and her eternal rewards and that change of focus helped her cope with the challenging circumstances that she lived with daily. Josh, Sam, Hannah and I found release in the power of forgiveness. Wilmot and Hannah's birth mother found that forgiving themselves can lead to a release and power that they didn't know was there.

We learned that the secret to forgiving others, ourselves and God is to be honest with ourselves and change our prayers by asking God to do a work in our own hearts first. My prayer for you is that you will find the power and release that comes with forgiveness and that God will use that to help you better fulfill the perfect plans that He has for you. An eternal focus will reap eternal rewards.

Life Application: WEST

1. What did you learn about heaven from Marcia's story? What do you think your accommodations will be like when you arrive in the afterlife?

2. What do you think of Billy's $2 bill philosophy from the *Unconditional* clips? Based on what you learned from this chapter, why is it true that no trial can take the Son away? Have you seen God bless you or others through a tough trial? Explain.

3. What have you been able to overcome that can help others who may be going through that very issue now? Look up *James 1:12* and reflect on what it means for you in your life? Will you receive a crown of life and/or a crown of glory when you get to heaven?

4. Look up *Colossians 3:13*. Reflect on the four words that we learned about from the chapel scene in *October Baby* as they relate to your own life: power, choice, burden and free.

5. Have you ever seen anyone transformed by the love of Christ like Wilmot McDowell was in the *Undaunted* film? Was it you? Share your story. Practicing sharing stories of victory and praising God for what He has done are powerful tools for helping others heal.

6. What did you learn from the opportunity to read your own story in the How to Set the Captives Free section? Is there an action step that you can take to move toward freedom and forgiveness? What commitment can you make today to set the captive free?

SOUTH
Leveraging Life Circumstances to Share your Faith and Light

    Standing up for God takes courage. Esther from the Bible knew this well. In 479 BC, King Xerxes I of Persia held a Cinderella-like ball to find a replacement for Queen Vashti, who had behaved disrespectfully and was banished. All the eligible bachelorettes of the day were summoned to the royal harem. The King found favor with Esther and he made her Queen. She was a young and beautiful Jewish woman who had been raised by her uncle Mordecai because she was orphaned at a young age. No one knew that Esther was a Jew. Haman, the King's right-hand man, despised Mordecai. So much so that Haman convinced the King to issue an irrevocable edict that called for the killing of all people of Jewish decent.

    Mordecai came to the palace to speak to Esther about the ramifications of this edict. He wanted her to know what would happen and she was in a unique position to do something about it. *Esther 4:14 New Living Translation (NLT), "If you keep quiet at a time like this, deliverance and relief for the Jews will arise from some other place, but you and your relatives will die.*

Who knows if perhaps you were made queen for just such a time as this?"

She had to talk with the King. Even though she was the Queen, this was a dangerous proposition. We can't look at this situation with present culture filters. If Esther walked in to the king's court unannounced the penalty was execution, unless the King extended his scepter of approval. She prayed and fasted for several days and asked other Jews to do the same. During that time, God gave her the plan. The King welcomed Esther and found favor with her.

The story ends with the bad guy hanging in the gallows and the Jews being saved. Esther found the strength and courage from God to allow Him to fulfill his plan for the rescue of the Jewish nation through her courageous obedience. I encourage you to read the whole exciting story in the book of Esther.

If you keep quiet about the truth of God's plan for people at a time like this, God will accomplish His will through someone else, but you will miss a blessing and maybe even your eternal reward.

Truth

There are four major ways that we can leverage our life circumstances to share the light and faith of Christ in this present culture:

- Know the truth
- Have the courage to tell the truth
- Lead people to the truth
- Live out the truth

Know the Truth

I was born to an upper middle-class Ohio family in the richest country in the world. It was a time where morals were just about to slip into a selfish spiral that would breed a spirit of rebellion, an entitlement mentality.

Today in America the prevailing messages that we learn from TV and other forms of media are things like:[31]

- Fathers are stupid.
- Women who don't have a professional job are less important than women who do.
- Disrespectful children are cute.
- Immorality is OK if you find a way to justify it.
- Religion and science are contradictory.
- Your dysfunctional upbringing defines the limits of your potential.
- It's OK to kill your unborn baby.
- Youth is better and more respectable than old age.
- Your circumstances and financial bottom line dictate your happiness.

Not long ago, even in this country, these messages would have been appalling. But to us, they are woven so tightly into the fabric of our cultural reality we don't even notice the messaging when we see it.

Your birth place, time and circumstances are critical environmental factors to your worldview. God placed you right where He did in the continuum of time for His good purposes.

He gave us the Bible as His unchanging ultimate truth to help us navigate the waters of life no matter what the world was telling us to believe. God wants us to be Holy, like Him. He wants us to shine His light and truth to a dark world.

What are some of the messages of truth in the Bible that Christians should be sharing and encouraging in our culture?

- God loves you.
- Children are a blessing.
- Life is precious at any age.
- Motherhood is noble and fulfilling.
- Strong loving fathers are the key to healthy families.
- Healthy families lead to a healthy society.
- Science explains God's world.
- God fully equips you for His great plans and purposes.
- Your weaknesses are your strengths.
- God can turn around any situation in life.
- God can free anyone from any bondage.
- You can find the power to overcome all circumstances through Christ.
- The Bible can guide us in all areas of our life.
- Wisdom from the Bible is unchanging and relevant to us today.
- All work is God honoring; no job is more important than any other.

God's truth is still God's truth. We need to spend time in the Word and in prayer as we have already discussed in the North section to know what that truth is so that we can recognize lies when we see them. Remember, this is not our home. We are citizens of heaven. Freedom from limiting beliefs is found in the Bible. The eternal perspective is necessary for us to have courage to face the trials and tribulations of this fallen world. *Hebrews 13:8, "Jesus Christ is the same yesterday, and today and forever."* He still wants the same thing that He always wanted — for us to have a relationship with Him and for us to live out the perfect plans He has for us.

Have the Courage to tell the Truth

There are a lot of reasons that Christians don't share their faith with others. Do you recognize these excuses in yourself?

- **Lack of knowledge:** I'm not a pastor or a Biblical scholar. What if someone asks me a question about God that I can't answer? I don't want to say the wrong thing.

- **Fear of judgment:** If I tell people that I am a Christian, they will expect me to be perfect. I'm not perfect and there are enough Christian hypocrites out there.

- **Location:** God is for Sundays at church. I can't talk about God at work. I will get fired.

- **Fear of what people will think:** I know that this person needs prayer, but if I offered to pray with them on the spot, they would probably think I was a freak.

- **Lack of conviction:** I don't want to push my faith on other people. It's not my business what they believe.

I have used all of these excuses and many more until I got some clarity about the differences between God's role in these circumstances and mine. Let's look at each of the examples above and break them down by roles and responsibilities.

- **Lack of Knowledge:**

It is your responsibility to learn about the Bible and continue to build your own personal relationship with Christ. True, years of Bible reading, and study will help make it easier to find and share helpful verses. But the *moment* that the Holy Spirit takes residence in a heart, He is present and all knowing. He will do the talking in all conversations if you ask Him to.

The minute a person asks me a question about the Bible or Jesus, I pray for God to give me scripture and words that will help and guide me. I may not know what book and verse to go to, but I can lead anyone to the Bible and some tools that will help them to find it for themselves. That one truth takes a load of responsibility off my shoulders and then I am free to be helpful. Wilmot McDowell didn't have time to become a Bible scholar and he still led scores of people to Christ in his last year of life.

- **Fear of Judgment:**

This is a big one. No human being has ever been perfect save for the Lord Jesus Christ. He alone is the standard for perfection, not his followers. God doesn't want Christians to pretend to be perfect. He wants us to be authentic. It is actually in our weakness and authenticity we are the most effective for the kingdom.

When you mess up, admit that you messed up. Model forgiveness and repentance in your own life and you will add credibility to your witness. Pride is the sin of hypocrites. Ask

God to help you peel off the layers of pride and you'll be more effective helping people fall in love with God. God's job is to be perfect and our job is to live authentically each day by His grace.

- **Location:**

The definition of integrity is to be whole and not divided; to be the same wherever you go. God doesn't want a compartmentalized heart. If you believe God in church on Sunday, then you believe God at work on Monday. I am not advocating you push tracts under people's noses at work or preach sermons at the lunch table. You can be a more effective witness by just doing your job with integrity or being gracious under pressure.

When you spend time with God you will become more like Him and people will ask you what water you are drinking. Make Jesus attractive to people by showing them that you have been transformed by Him. Don't push Jesus on people. Let people ask you about Jesus. Then, let the Holy Spirit do the talking. *Colossians 4:5-6 NLT, "Live wisely among those who are not believers, and make the most of every opportunity. Let your conversation be gracious and attractive so that you will have the right response for everyone."*

- **Fear of what People will Think:**

Prayer is one of the very best ways that you can shine your light. The Holy Spirit will let you know when a person really needs prayer. We will talk about how later in this chapter. God may want you to pray for a perfect stranger or a member of your family. If someone is hurting it is so powerful to ask if you can pray for them. It is even more powerful when you actually do. To say 'I'll pray for you" is good. But asking if you can pray for them right now shows you mean business. I have only been refused one time. People usually appreciate it when you pray and often comment later how much it helped to pray with them. I also love to hear reports of answered prayers. It's the Holy Spirit's job to prompt us to pray and it's our job to do it. You and the person you are praying for will be blessed. If you don't do it, you will miss a blessing and so will they.

- **Lack of Conviction:**

There are plenty of roles that people can play on the road to someone's decision for Christ. One person may have shared their own testimony, another lives their faith well. Some may lead you to the Bible and help understand the truths in it. Another may answer your questions or just spend time helping you understand God's plan for you. All of these roles are part of the salvation process. When someone is ready to receive Christ, they or the Holy Spirit will tell you they are ready. Regardless of the various roles people play along the way, the job of salvation is always the Holy Spirit's. You can't take credit or blame for anyone's decision. Salvation is a deal made one-on-one with the Holy Spirit.

We should never be pushy about our faith. It does not honor God to offend people with our witness. Our job is to spend time with God in the Word and in prayer so we can become more like Jesus. Then we can live out our faith in a way that makes Jesus attractive. The Holy Spirit's job is to lead, guide and show us the ways we can help others do the same.

One thing that many of these reasons have in common is "self." Self is the biggest barrier to the work of the Holy Spirit; self-consciousness, self-centeredness, selfish desires, self-deprecating thoughts, etc. The reason that "self" issues are a barrier to freedom and blocked the power of the Holy Spirit, is because the focus is on you and not on God's power, His love, His plans and kingdom purposes. Self-consciousness for example, is the root cause of the fear of what people think of you because your eyes are focused on seeking approval from others instead of seeking approval from God. When we learn how to begin with God rather than beginning with ourselves, the Lord can overcome every barrier.

Lead People to the Truth- Clip 1 from King's Faith

One of the simplest ways to share your faith is by telling your story. There is nothing more powerful than an authentic God-transforming testimony. If God has changed you, share your victory with others.

There are two different clips relevant to this chapter from the *King's Faith* film. Brendan King has spent his young life bouncing between 18 different foster homes and, most recently, 3 years in jail. Let's watch how Brendan shares his testimony and vision with a group of teens he met doing community service.

King's Faith 1

http://bit.ly/1ccNTVR [32]

See PattySadallah.com Other Books tab Paperback Film Links, King's Faith 1

If you break down Brendan's 'presentation' you can simply follow the same model for sharing your own testimony.

Brendan began by *sharing where he used to be*. He shared the story of that house. How the foster kids became his gang and that they got in trouble with drugs and violence. He shared that he lost a close friend right where they were standing and that he too had nearly been killed.

Then he shared *who intervened* and what they did. He told of the prison chaplain that offered him a Bible. He shared that reading that Bible *changed him*. Brendan accepted Christ and God began to change his heart.

Then he shared *what he wanted to do*. God put a vision on his heart and he knew what God wanted him to do. He didn't know how to go about rehabbing that house so that he could make a safe haven for kids in the neighborhood. But he wanted to share the love of Christ there. He *shared about God's character*. He got the kids to *see it and want it, too*.

He also showed his own faith and character when he said, "I have a vision, I just have to step into it." *Matthew 19:26, "Jesus looked at them and said, "With man this is impossible, but with God all things are possible."* Brendan told them, "If God can give me a second chance, He can do just about anything."

Brendan was casual. He was authentic. He was humble and he knew that he owed God a debt of gratitude for what God had done for him. He wanted to pass on the blessings. That is really what it is all about.

Live out the Truth- Clip 2 from Kings Faith

King's Faith 2

http://bit.ly/1blSxQe [33]

See PattySadallah.com Other Books tab Paperback Film Links, King's Faith 2

Can you relate to Brendan in this clip from *King's Faith*? He's in a big mess and he's trying to fix it on his own with limited options and resources. Mike is Brendan's 18th foster parent but he is the first one to have courage to lead him to the truth. Mike tells Brandon that he is not fighting a flesh and blood fight, but one with the powers of darkness. *Ephesians 6:12, "For our struggle is not against flesh and blood, but against the rulers, against the authorities, against the powers of this dark world and against the spiritual forces of evil in the heavenly realms."* Mike tells Brendan that the enemy is afraid of what he can become if he finds victory in this situation. That's why it is so important to turn everything over to God. Mike shared one of the most classic of all memory verses, *Proverbs 3:5-6*

> "[5] *Trust in the Lord with all your heart*
>
> *and lean not on your own understanding;*
>
> [6] *in all your ways submit to Him,*
>
> *and He will make your paths straight. [a]"*

Mike demonstrated the power of knowing the truth, having the courage to tell the truth and how to use it to help someone in trouble. Pastor Charles Eduardos does this better than anyone I have ever met. Along with being a Pastor, he is also the "Victory Mind Mapper," a life coach whose mission is to help people live out *Romans 12:2. "Do not conform to the pattern of this world but be transformed by the renewing of your mind. Then you will be able to test and approve what God's will is—His good, pleasing and perfect will."*

Charles was in my group when I was leading a Truth at Work Roundtable in Cleveland. It was an accountability group for people to learn how to live out their faith in the workplace. Someone would say something that was limiting or defeating related to a challenge or circumstance and Charles would say; "Is that true? Because my Bible says..." and he would whip out a perfect scripture for the circumstance. It was an instant reframe for everyone in the room. In all cases, God is bigger than our challenges and circumstances.

Put on the Full Armor of God

The Bible gives us instruction on how to protect ourselves from the schemes of the enemy and how to fight back with the full armor of God.

Ephesians 6:10-18:

> "*¹⁰ Finally, be strong in the Lord and in His mighty power. ¹¹ Put on the full armor of God, so that you can take your stand against the devil's schemes. ¹² For our struggle is not against flesh and blood, but against the rulers, against the authorities, against the powers of this dark world and against the spiritual forces of evil in the heavenly realms. ¹³ Therefore put on the full armor of God, so that when the day of evil comes, you may be able to stand your ground, and after you have done everything, to stand. ¹⁴ Stand firm then, with the **belt of truth** buckled around your waist, with the **breastplate of righteousness** in place, ¹⁵ and with your **feet fitted** with the readiness that comes from the **gospel of peace**. ¹⁶ In addition to all this, take up the **shield of faith**, with which you can extinguish all the flaming arrows of the evil one. ¹⁷ Take the **helmet of salvation** and the **sword of the Spirit**, which is the word of God.*
>
> *¹⁸ And **pray in the Spirit** on all occasions with all kinds of prayers and requests. With this in mind, be alert and always keep on praying for the entire Lord's people." (bold emphasis mine)*

The full armor of God was a metaphor that would have been easily understood in the day it was written. Soldiers wore armor for protection in battle. There was no covering for the back because soldiers marched forward and if they turned their backs, it was a form of treason; there was no protection for treason. It's a good reminder for us that when we turn our backs on God, we are forfeiting His protection. But, when we fight our battles with God, we have His full protection and He is doing the fighting for us. Let's look at the individual pieces of the armor.

The **belt of truth** holds all the armor in place and represents sincerity, authenticity, and pure motives.

The **breastplate of righteousness** is Christ's righteousness, our heart covering. It protects our hearts from the lies that try to penetrate and steal our victories.

Feet fitted with the gospel of peace, represents our willingness to walk with Christ by faith. It's our ability to stand our ground and march toward being Christ-like.

The **shield of faith** believes God for His promises amidst trials and temptations.

The **helmet of salvation** is wisdom and discernment that comes from spending time in the Word and knowledge of the difference between Biblical truth and Satan's lies.

The **sword of the Spirit** is the Holy Word of God and the only offensive weapon. The other armor pieces are protection. Speaking Bible truth sends the enemy packing. Remember to pray out loud if you are fighting a spiritual battle.

Prayer in the Spirit means praying God's will. It is agreeing with the Holy Spirit's perfect prayers for you in every situation. When you don't know what to pray, simply ask God to show you or pray in agreement with the Holy Spirit.

It's also important to remember that God will fight your battles for you, like Mike reminded Brendan. *2 Chronicles 20:17, "You will not have to fight this battle. Take up your positions; stand firm and see the deliverance the LORD will give you, Judah and Jerusalem. Do not be afraid; do not be discouraged. Go out to face them tomorrow, and the LORD will be with you.'"*

Exodus 14:14, "The LORD will fight for you; you need only to be still."

Ready Yourself to Share the Truth- Clip from Seklas Seeds

The seed in this film, *Seklas Seeds* represents the transformational living Word of God. This film was set in WWII Nazi Germany. This is a time when evil people were trying to destroy God's chosen people. Did you know that the devil is not all knowing? Only God is omniscient. Satan doesn't know when Jesus will return any more than we do, so he needs to raise up an anti-Christ in every generation to be ready for the final battle. I believe Hitler was one of those being prepared for the job. The enemy will always try to destroy the Word by using evil people. But the Word of God can't be destroyed. It lives on generation after generation.

Seklas Seeds

http://bit.ly/19yV22o [34]

See PattySadallah.com Other Books tab Paperback Film Links, Seklas Seeds

Let's address some obvious observations about the film before we dig into some of its hidden spiritual nuggets. Did you notice the overall lack of joy this scientist had with his life and job at the beginning of the film? The scientist's job was to destroy the seed, but it had a baffling and even sometimes amusing resiliency. After the seed started to grow and the scientist began to share it, there was real joy! That's exactly what it's like when you begin to share the Word of God with others.

A seed is a metaphor for the Christian Life. Like a cell in the human body, a seed has the complete genetic code needed to become what it was designed to become. In its initial form, it doesn't look like much, and it certainly does not look like what it has the potential to become. Like the seed embryo, we ALL have a divine potential that God has planned for us.

> *Jeremiah 29:11-13 reminds us that God has a plan for all of us. "For I know the plans I have for you," declares the Lord, "plans to prosper you and not to harm you, plans to give you hope and a future. Then you will call on me and come and pray to me, and I will listen to you. You will seek me and find me when you seek me with all your heart."*

The conditions need to be right before we can to be ready for that future. For some, the conditions are hitting rock bottom in a life of progressive, habitual sin. For others it may be realizing that there must be something better for them than a boring humdrum existence. Some cry out in the midst of tragic life circumstances and others are just gradually made ready by the prayers of loved ones or steady deposits of the Word's messages of hope. Regardless of circumstantial differences, a softening of the hard shell of our hearts needs to occur. We must admit that we need God. We must accept His grace. It requires a death of self to soften and break open that hard shell.

Jesus tells us in *John 12:24, "Very truly I tell you, unless a kernel of wheat falls to the ground and dies, it remains only a single seed. But if it dies, it produces many seeds. So, we must die to ourselves to find the joy."*

Farmers know seeds need good soil, sunlight, water, weeding and time to grow into fruit-bearing crops. With the right conditions, a tiny seed can produce food with hundreds of seeds. Which brings me to the next cool spiritual insight from this clip: God is the God of multiplication! He is not a God of addition or subtraction. Healthy soil can produce a crop 100 times what was sown. Think about what the world would look like if *every* Christian truly prepared their hearts, drank deeply the Living Water, spent time in prayer and conversation with God and allowed Him to fulfill their divine purposes to 100 times what they labored! It certainly would be a completely different world!

To take this seed metaphor just a bit farther, let's look at the Christian life like you were a successful farmer.

Soil- nourishment:

The soil is a critical component to a healthy plant and a healthy Christian life. Jesus shared this truth in the parable of the sower in *Matthew 13, ³"Then He told them many things in parables, saying: "A farmer went out to sow His seed. ⁴ As he was scattering the seed, some fell along the path, and the birds came and ate it up. ⁵ Some fell on rocky places, where it did not have much soil. It sprang up quickly, because the soil was shallow. ⁶ But when the sun came up, the plants were scorched, and they withered because* they had no root. ⁷ Other seed fell among thorns, which grew up and choked the plants. ⁸ Still other seed fell on good soil, where it produced a crop—a hundred, sixty or thirty times what was sown. ⁹ Whoever has ears, let them hear."

Jesus explained what these verses meant in *Matthew 13:18-23*

> ¹⁸ "Listen then to what the parable of the sower means: ¹⁹ When anyone hears the message about the kingdom and does not understand it, the evil one comes and snatches away what was sown in their heart. This is the seed sown along the path. ²⁰ The seed falling on rocky ground refers to someone who hears the word and at once receives it with joy. ²¹ But since they have no root, they last only a short time. When trouble or persecution comes because of the word, they quickly fall away. ²² The seed falling among the thorns refers to someone who hears the word, but the worries of this life and the deceitfulness of wealth choke the word, making it unfruitful. ²³ But the seed falling on good soil refers to someone who hears the word and understands it. This is the one who produces a crop, yielding a hundred, sixty or thirty times what was sown."

Make sure your heart has healthy soil. Spend time daily in the Word and learn more about what it means. This will keep your heart fed with truth. Reading Bible commentaries, Christian books and being in Bible study will keep the soil of your heart fertile for continued growth.

Sunlight- encouragement:

Surround yourself with people who believe in God, you and your mission. Let them shed the warm sunshine of encouragement to give you energy for the work. Be sunshine for others as well. God is the Comforter and there are so many encouraging verses in the Bible. Really immerse yourself in these scriptures. Every life has its difficult seasons and we were never meant to navigate our lives alone.

Living Water- revitalization:

Water is necessary for life. We can live without food for much longer than we can live without water. Water refreshes, revitalizes and brings health to plants and the body. The Living Water is the Holy Spirit within each believer. He is always there and is ready to revitalize us. But we need to acknowledge Him with prayer to receive His full benefits. The Holy Spirit revitalizes our soul and makes sense of the Word of God for us. He is called the Comforter and the Helper. It is through our prayer conversations and time with God that we engage the Holy Spirit in our lives and can be refreshed and renewed.

Jesus taught us about living water when He spoke to the woman at the well. In response to the woman's question about how she could give Jesus a drink from the well without a ladle Jesus instructs us in *John 4: 10-14:*

> *"$_{10}$ Jesus answered her, "If you knew the gift of God and who it is that asks you for a drink, you would have asked Him and He would have given you living water." $_{11}$ "Sir," the woman said, "you have nothing to draw with and the well is deep. Where can you*

> *get this living water?* $_{12}$ *Are you greater than our father Jacob, who gave us the well and drank from it himself, as did also his sons and his livestock?"* $_{13}$ *Jesus answered, "Everyone who drinks this water will be thirsty again,* $_{14}$ *but whoever drinks the water I give them will never thirst. Indeed, the water I give them will become in them a spring of water welling up to eternal life."*

As long as you continue to have access to that living water, we will continue to grow into the person that God has created you to become.

Fertilizing: learn from life's challenges:

The manure in life is there to fertilize. Fertilization occurs when we learn from the challenging lessons of life. We have already covered this in the West chapter. When God brings us through a challenge, we are more equipped to serve and help others. By sharing what we have learned, we can encourage people and show them the way to freedom. We are more useful to the kingdom healed than we would be sick in our sins or having lived an unchallenged life.

Weeding- purging of negativity:

Weeds choke out healthy crops and are fruitless. They quickly grow out of control, just like negative thoughts. Don't let negativity creep into your thought life because it will quickly kill off your dreams and kingdom impact. *2 Corinthians 10:5a says "We demolish arguments and every pretension that sets itself up against the knowledge of God, and we take captive every thought to make it obedient to Christ."* Take negative thoughts captive and you will weed the garden of your heart and stay on track for God's perfect plan for you.

Time- patience:

Can you imagine a farmer going out one day and planting some seeds and then one week later being disappointed that there was no crop? Success takes time. Work on your Christian walk every day. God doesn't measure the outcome, He measures your journey. God wants to see you seeking Him and walking obediently every day.

Don't dig up your seeds

If a farmer were to plant a seed and then dig it up a few days later to see what was going on under the earth, it would not grow properly. Likewise, don't let your impatience get you off track. God prepares us day-by-day for our blessings and His perfect plans. We can lose our way quickly by getting ahead of God. Listen to the Holy Spirit's voice and He will get you where He wants you to go in perfect timing. God's plans are wiser than ours, so we need to let God be in control of how He decides to keep His promises. Don't dig up your seeds. Listen closely to God's plan for you and follow it closely. Continue to stay in contact with God and He will lead you to that plan that He has specifically designed for you. Remember, it is a plan to prosper you and give you a future. It's a plan of multiplication and blessings.

How to Follow God's Lead: God Speaks Clip

At first look, this video may seem a bit ridiculous. I mean God doesn't communicate to us like He did to Doug in this *God*

Speaks video. Does He? I didn't realize until later in my spiritual journey how much God actually does speak to us that directly.

God Speaks

http://bit.ly/2BtaW2M [35]

See PattySadallah.com Other Books tab Paperback Film Links, God Speaks

I was having one of those days where I had a big list of "to do's" but God had other plans. It was the week I began writing this chapter and I guess God thought I needed a personal illustration for it. My daughter Jamael's car is a black Toyota Corolla named Dolores. Yes, Jamael named her car. While I was running through my errands, I kept seeing Dolores look-alike cars passing by. It took about the fourth Dolores for me to get that God probably wanted me to pray for Jamael.

I prayed a general blessing for her. Then saw two more black Toyota Corollas on the road. It was so weird. Each time I saw Dolores, I would pray for Jamael. At about the third prayer I realized I needed to also pray for Dolores. I needed to pray for safety on the road. Oddly enough, I got a flat tire while praying for her safety; so much for my plans for that day.

God put a sweet elderly man in my path. He just happened to be pumping gas at the station I managed to drive to before the tire got too flat. He kindly changed the tire to my spare. God was demonstrating how an act of kindness shows the love of Christ through this man's timely help.

While the tire was getting fixed, I saw another Dolores and said another prayer. The spare tire wasn't holding air, so I had to drive it to a tire place to get a new one. While I was at the repair shop, I saw another Dolores, and said another prayer.

When I was finally on my way home, I got a call from Jamael. She called to tell me she had just escaped a near accident on the highway. A man was driving recklessly and nearly hit her car. If she hadn't seen him racing diagonally in her rearview mirror, she would've been in a serious accident. I told her about all the Dolores twins on the road and all the prayers and we agreed it was a miracle. Those prayers prevented an accident.

I encountered nine black Toyota Corollas in the same day! Was it just a coincidence? I don't believe in coincidences, I believe in God-incidences. God orchestrated the lives of nine drivers to pass by me just so I could pray for Jamael's safety and share this story. None of them will ever know that they played a role in answering a prayer of safety for my daughter.

Over the next few days I looked for black Toyota Corollas everywhere I drove. I wondered if I naturally drove by that many and just never noticed. I believe that even if I had driven by that many black Toyota Corollas every day, it would have still been a message from God, because I had never noticed them before. But, it was worth the research. On the first day I saw two Toyota Corollas; neither one was black. I didn't see any on the second day, and on the third day, I saw one black and one silver one.

What do you think would have happened if I hadn't noticed those cars or prayed as God was prompting me? I'm not exactly sure. I think it was God's will that she be saved from that accident, and if I hadn't prayed, He may have used someone else on the road to pray for her or she made have cried out in prayer herself. I do know one thing for sure though. If I hadn't prayed for her, I would have missed the blessing and you would've missed the blessing because you never would have heard about it.

The Holy Spirit communicates to us all day long. *John 14:26 Amplified Bible (AMP), "But the Comforter (Counselor, Helper, Intercessor, Advocate, Strengthener, Standby), the Holy Spirit, Whom the Father will send in my name [in my place, to represent me and act on my behalf], He will teach you all things. And He will cause you to recall (will remind you of, bring to your remembrance) everything I have told you."* The Holy Spirit has a lot to teach us and desires to keep us on track for God's will in our lives.

And according to *John 16:13 Amplified Bible (AMP), "But when He, the Spirit of Truth (the Truth-giving Spirit) comes, He will guide you into all the Truth (the whole, full Truth). For He will not speak His own message [on His own authority]; but He will tell whatever He hears [from the Father; He will give the message that has been given to Him], and He will announce and declare to you the things that are to come [that will happen in the future]."*

We need to listen to the leadings and messages of the Holy Spirit when He is trying to show us something. We need to cooperate with the Holy Spirit, or we will miss out on blessings and opportunities to bless others.

If God doesn't email us or flash messages specifically for us on a billboard like He did for Doug in the film clip, then how does the Holy Spirit communicate with us and how can we know that the messages are actually from Him? The Holy Spirit speaks to us through these forms of heavenly correspondence:

The **Word of God** is alive. The Holy Spirit can bring a scripture to mind or lead you to the exact verse you need. He can also reveal the meaning of a verse in a fresh and new way, speaking to your current circumstance.

A **quickening or jump** is when God gets your attention and causes you to stop and notice. That's what He did with the Dolores. Sometimes jumps can be associated with an uneasy feeling or can even cause physical discomfort. When you feel this, take a moment to pray for the Holy Spirit to give you clarity in what you should pray about or do at that moment.

Promptings or leadings are when you are given direction. *Romans 8:14, "14 For those who are led by the Spirit of God are the children of God."* The Holy Spirit knows the plans God has for you and He knows the future. He knows the way to go and He endeavors to communicate direction to us with promptings and leadings. He will give you an inner knowing or an assurance of a direction. Sometimes this direction can feel like a gentle breeze and sometimes it feels as obvious as a hurricane. The more you stay in the Word and in prayer, the more you will be able to discern God's leadings from your own desires. We will talk more about this one in the East chapter when we address callings from God.

A **quiet still voice** is when you hear God's voice. Not necessarily audibly, but it's not your own inner voice and you know it. My mother had a healing from cancer many years ago. She was at a healing service and she heard God say in her spirit, "You are healed my child." That's not something you say to yourself. Her cancer counts dropped from over 500 to single digits by the next checkup. The doctors were stumped. But not as much as they were when they conducted the follow-up surgery and there was no scar tissue from the original surgery. God confirmed His message. She was healed!

Knowing in your Spirit is when "you know that you know that you know" what God is telling you. This comes with a spiritual maturity that increases as you spend time in the Word of God and in prayer. You just know what God wants you to do. You just know where He wants you to go. This kind of discernment comes with time and patience.

You will know that a **dream** is from the Holy Spirit if you can remember it clearly and you know that God is trying to tell you something from it. It may take some prayer and some time, but God will reveal its meaning if you pray for clarity. The dream that Tim had where He encountered God was an example of how the Holy Spirit can use a dream to put a life back on track.

A **check in your spirit** is an intuition that warns you of danger. It can also be a way to avoid a sin trap. They can feel like stop signs, demanding that you pause and take notice of something. It is always wise to obey these warning signs. There will be uneasiness or even a guilt feeling if you ignore a check in your spirit.

Visions are when you get a picture in your mind's eye that makes something clear. God gave me a vision of the model and details of this book with pictures, words and diagrams. When God gives you a vision, carefully write down what you saw and pray for wisdom and discernment for what it means and what He wants you to do with it.

You can initiate these visionary encounters with Jesus at any time. I have already mentioned the Special Place exercise earlier in the book. God is ready 24/7 to meet with you in your Special Place. He will speak to you by name and show you exactly what you need to understand. I ask Jesus to help me understand people's hearts, or scripture, or issues related to my life. He often gives me metaphors to help make something clear, of just gives me peace in my heart. He is always there waiting and as He said to a student of mine, Isabelle, about her Special Place:

What Jesus said to Isabelle about her Special Place:

> "My LORD, please make me more sensitive to Your Presence in my heart. How You feel, how You see things, how You move and how You transform me. I want this permanent awareness of Your presence my LORD, just like the first days after my rebirth, remember Father? I'll never forget that! I want it back LORD, increasingly more and on a deeper level. Would you grant me this LORD, I need You to be much more prominent in my life, more of You LORD and less of me."

> *"My dear child, this is a good longing, which will change your life. You remember your first love and my response to it. Let Me renew your first love for Me, let's start by meeting each other every day in that special*

> *place of yours. I know exactly where it is. I do love you so much my child and I can't tell you how much*

> *I'd love to share with you. I'd like to take you all over the world, show you the wonders of My creation, show you my children, there's so many I'd like you to meet and have fellowship with. What do you say Isabelle?*

"When do we leave LORD? My suitcases are packed whenever You say LORD! I loooove it!"

"How about now?"

Prophecies are direct messages from God. They are given to people who have the Spiritual Gift of prophecy. It is important to test every message that you think is prophetic against the Word of God. *Hebrews 13:8* instructs us, *"Jesus Christ is the same yesterday and today and forever."* If someone says that they have a message from God and it doesn't line up with Holy Scripture, it is not from the Holy Spirit. God still gives people the spiritual gift of prophecy today. The message to Tim about the overcoat is an example of a prophetic message from God.

Prophecy is not fortune telling. All people can hear God's voice because He created us with that capability. It simply means hearing from God and sharing what He said. Dialogue Journaling is a tool that allows you to use 4 simple keys to hear the fine-tuning dial of God's voice more clearly so you can record your conversations like Isabelle did. It is remarkably simple.

- Just quiet yourself down,
- fix your eyes on Jesus,
- tune to positive spontaneous thoughts, feelings, pictures and emotions,
- and write them down,

The *Just Ask Jesus* book series shares more on dialogue journaling, but for more information now, here is an 8-minute video by Dr. Mark Virkler, President of CLU explaining the 4 Keys to Hearing God's Voice. https://bit.ly/2SlpHiD [45]

God speaks to us in all these ways. The closer you are to God, the more you will be able to discern His messages and find confidence in what His will is for your life. The more you include God in your life and decisions, the more you can leverage life circumstances to share your faith and live out His plan.

The Romans Road

The book of Romans is a great place to start for people to understand God's plan. These verses are typically considered the Romans Road. Memorize these few verses and you can explain the Good News of Jesus Christ to anyone who is seeking Him.

- **All have sinned-** *Romans 3:10, "As it is written: There is no one righteous, not even one;"* and *Romans 3:23, "for all have sinned and fall short of the glory of God,"*

- **Penalty of sin-** *Romans 5:12, "Therefore, just as sin entered the world through one man, and death through sin, and in this way death came to all men, because all sinned."* And *Romans 6:23, "For the wages of sin is death, but the gift of God is eternal life in Christ Jesus our Lord."*

- **Christ paid the penalty for our sin-** *Romans 5:8, "But God demonstrates His own love for us in this: While we were still sinners, Christ died for us."*

- **We are saved by faith-** *Romans 10:9-10, "That if you confess with your mouth, "Jesus is Lord," and believe in your heart that God raised Him from the dead, you will* be saved. $_{10}$ For it is with your heart that you believe and are justified, and it is with your mouth that you confess and are saved." And Romans 10:13, "Everyone who calls on the name of the Lord will be saved."

Don't worry about what to say. If God has asked you to speak to someone, submit your mouth to Him and let Him speak through you.

Be the Moon

God is the Light and as Christians, we are the reflection of His light. *Matthew 5:14-16 says, "$_{14}$ You are the light of the world. A town built on a hill cannot be hidden. $_{15}$ Neither do people light a lamp and put it under a bowl. Instead they put it on its stand, and it gives light to everyone in the house. $_{16}$ In the same way, let your light shine before others, that they may see your good deeds and glorify your Father in heaven."*

God is the sun. Christians are to be the moon, reflecting His light in the world. What are ways that we can reflect God's light daily?

Be considerate. Really see people. Acknowledge the 'invisible' people who serve you in the checkout lines, direct traffic on the street, etc. Be polite, open a door or help a stranger who looks like they need a hand.

Be faithful. Offer to pray with someone if they are having a bad day. Tell people you will pray for them and really do it! Act on promptings to call and check in on people that God puts on your heart. Pray for rude people; they have a story you don't know about. Create conversational opportunities to share where you get your peace. Give God the credit when people ask you 'how do you do it?'

Be grateful. Thank people for what they do for you. Send a thoughtful note or card to encourage or show appreciation.

Be friendly. Make someone laugh, especially on a day that they look like they need to laugh. Smile at people because smiling is contagious.

Be joyful. Sing a Christian song joyfully as you go about your day.

Be patient. When you are going through something tough, model your faith by showing grace and peace in tough times so that people will ask how you cope with pressures so well. Be patient because patience is not common in a frustrating situation.

Life Application: SOUTH

1. What did you learn about God's truth?

2. In what way does fear keep you from sharing your faith?

3. Reflecting on the steps Brendan used to share His testimony in the *King's Faith* clip; journal out your own testimony using these steps: Where did you used to be? Who intervened to help you? How are you changed? What has God put on your heart to do?

4. Journal a prayer using the Full Armor of God and place it somewhere you see often like the refrigerator or your bathroom mirror. Make it a practice to pray it often.

5. Looking at the Romans Road scriptures, practice how you may share the message of salvation with someone. *Romans 3:10, 5:12, 5:8,* and *10:9-10.*

6. What can you do to multiply your impact from the ideas you got from the Seed clip and the farming section?

7. How do you hear from God? What will you do to hear from God more often and more clearly?

8. What are ways you can be the moon this week?

EAST
Use your Gifts to Bless Others & Advance the Kingdom

"I may be here for a short while, gone tomorrow into oblivion or until the days come to take me away. But, in whatever part you play, be remembered as part of a legacy... of sharing dreams and changing humanity for the better. It's that legacy that never dies." Unknown.

"*M*akin' memories and changin' lives"... That's what Doug, our fast-talking, long-haired white-water rafting guide said was his purpose in life and he surely lives it! When on vacation in the West Virginia New River Gorge, our family signed up for the rafting adventure and Doug had 20 minutes to prepare us for what would be one of the coolest experiences I have ever had. He talked so fast I could hardly process his words. But in that brief time, he told stories, gave us key safety instructions, told more cow jokes than I thought existed and had me smiling the entire time. He *loved* his work and was very clear about his mission in life. He knew that he played a key role in the making of the perfect vacation and family experience. His work was about us, the vacationers, never about himself.

I started thinking about Doug and the legacy that he is leaving; the impact that he had on me whether he was aware of it or not. I realize that we all leave a legacy, good or bad, intentionally or unintentionally. We are all being observed by others and those observations lead to indelible impressions in people's minds. Doug's legacy was shining the light of Christ.

God sends the Holy Spirit to every believer and fully equips them to live out the perfect plan He has for each of us. He calls some into formal ministry, but most of us are to serve by our life example, regardless of our occupations. All work is Holy if you do it with honor, integrity and as a service to the Lord. *2 Timothy 2:20-21 (MSG), "In a well-furnished kitchen there are not only crystal goblets and silver platters, but waste cans and compost buckets—some containers used to serve fine meals, others to take out the garbage. Become the kind of container God can use to present any and every kind of gift to His guests for their blessing."* It's not the type of work, but how you do it, that blesses people and makes it God-honoring.

Work is Worship Clip

With more than 800 verses in the Bible about work, God has a lot to say about it. *Colossians 3:23* says, *"Whatever you do, work at it with all your heart, as working for the Lord, not for human masters."* This *Work is Worship* clip will shed light on what God thinks about work. What would change if you really thought of the Lord as your boss?

Work is Worship

http://bit.ly/13AgscN [36]

PattySadallah.com Other Books tab Paperback Film Links, Work is Worship

As adults, most of our waking time is spent at work. Many will admit they spend more time with coworkers than they do with their own families. I don't think it's ever God's plan for us to dread our work, yet so many of us do. Maybe your work conditions are horrendous. You may have an unpleasant work environment or tedious job. But if you're doing your work as a service to the Lord, it changes your perspective.

My father spent only a few days in a hospice nursing facility before he passed away. I remember a nurse that worked there and a particularly unpleasant dementia patient in the next room. This patient was cranky, mean and ungrateful; no doubt an unfortunate side effect of her disease. I watched this nurse serve her with so much joy and patience. I wondered how this nurse could cope with those daily challenges and still maintain such a great attitude. I remember saying something to her about how difficult the job seems and how impressed

I was with her level of patience. I remember her saying, "I'm not working for her approval. I'm working for the Lord." She didn't need her patients to appreciate what she was doing. Her reward came from knowing she was doing the will of the Father.

If God is the boss we are accountable to today, it makes us more aware of the everyday encounters and opportunities God puts in our path to serve others with our gifts. Jesus chose fishermen, a doctor, a tent maker and a tax collector to be His apostles. *John 6:28-29, "Then they asked Him, 'What must we do to do the works God requires?' $_{29}$Jesus answered, 'The work of God is this: to believe in the one He has sent.'"* Jesus chose ordinary men living and working in the marketplace to spread the good news of salvation. Keep asking the question, "What would God want me to do today?" Set aside your own agenda for the day and see if God's plan is different. After all, shouldn't we be working as part of God's plan and not having God come along side our plans?

When our decisions are guided by the Lord, He will bless them. When our heart seeks to please God, work will become more joyful and rewarding. You don't have to be an ordained minister to have a ministry. When I was working for Truth at Work, CEO Ray Hilbert used to say, "When you meet someone and they ask you what you do for a living, tell them that you're a Kingdom Builder cleverly disguised as (fill in your job title here). It's a great conversation starter and they will know who your Boss is."

God wants all of you. He doesn't want you to just think about Him on Sundays, but always. God had a plan for you before you were even born. *Psalm 139:12-14:*

> "$_{12}$ even the darkness will not be dark to you;
>
> the night will shine like the day,
>
> for darkness is as light to you.
>
> $_{13}$ For you created my inmost being;
>
> you knit me together in my mother's womb.
>
> $_{14}$ I praise you because I am fearfully and wonderfully made;
>
> your works are wonderful,
>
> I know that full well."

The plans for you are connected to God's bigger plan for others and for the whole world. When God created you, He wired you with a unique personality, experiences, abilities, interests and passions. When you are saved, He gives you spiritual gifts. When you add a desire to serve God according to His purposes, you have the recipe for true fulfillment in life. Realizing Jesus is the boss and seeking to please Him will help you find joy in serving. That's the secret of leaving a God-honoring legacy.

What determines whether our legacy will be positive or negative? My hypothesis is that selflessness leads to a positive legacy and selfishness leads to a negative legacy. Test this out as I have in my own life. Think about the heroes in your life; the people who have left the most positive lasting impression on you. Were they selfless? My list sure was. Now, think about those people who leave a bad taste in your memory mouth. Were they selfish? Yep, mine too.

We truly can't be selfless without the Holy Spirit. Left to our own devices, we are all selfish. *Philippians 2:3* reminds us, *"Do nothing out of selfish ambition or vain conceit. Rather, in humility value others above yourselves."*

If you want to have more impact in your work and your mission in life, put God and others ahead of yourself. Serve for their benefit, not for your own. Not only will you have more success in work and life, but you will make a difference in the world. You will leave a positive legacy. Examine your motives. Are you just working to make money? Or do you believe that what you are doing is really helping people and glorifying God?

He can use you too

Isaiah 6:8, "Then I heard the Lord asking, 'Whom should I send as a messenger to this people? Who will go for us?' I said, 'Here I am. Send me.'"

As a follower of Christ, God has big plans for your kingdom impact. You have the chance to improve your eternal rewards and heavenly residence by following God for those big plans. God uniquely equips each of us for the ministry impact that He desires for us. Will you have the courage to do what God calls you to do?

If you are like me, you can feel unqualified and scared to take on challenges that God asks of you. You may claim your weaknesses as an excuse for not serving the way God has intended. In fact, God loves to show His strength through our weaknesses. The Apostle Paul confirms this truth in *2 Corinthians 12:9, "But He said to me, 'My grace is sufficient for you, for my power is made perfect in weakness.' Therefore, I will boast all the more gladly about my weaknesses, so that Christ's power may rest on me."*

Pastor Jonathan Schaeffer said it so well one Sunday in the church bulletin that I just had to pass it on to you:

From: "A note from Jonathan" June 24, 2012 [37]

"A lot of us feel inadequate for the assignments that God gives us. In fact, you may be uninvolved in serving right now because you don't think you have what it takes. God wants to use you! The truth is, He's always shown His strength through people who have made excuses but finally made themselves available to Him.

- Abraham was old.
- Jacob was insecure.
- Leah was unattractive.
- Joseph was abused.
- Moses stuttered.
- Gideon was poor,
- Samson was co-dependent.
- Rahab was immoral.
- David had an affair and all kinds of family problems.
- Elijah was suicidal.
- Jeremiah was depressed,
- Jonah was reluctant.
- Naomi was a widow.
- John the Baptist was eccentric . . . to say the least.
- Peter was impulsive and hot-tempered.

- Martha worried a lot.
- The Samaritan woman had several failed marriages.
- Zaccheaeus was unpopular.
- Thomas had doubts.
- Paul had poor health.
- Timothy was timid.

That's quite a variety of misfits, but God used each of them in His service. He will use all of us, too, when we stop making excuses." ~Jonathan Schaeffer, Senior Pastor, Grace Church, CMA.

So if you feel flawed, inadequate or overwhelmed, you are in good company. God loves to use imperfect people to advance the kingdom. Has God laid something on your heart? Perhaps He wants you to change jobs or move to another city. Maybe it's time to take the plunge and get married. Maybe you feel the tug to volunteer at a local nonprofit organization or just reach out to your neighbors. If you feel that heart tug, God will be with you when you step out in faith. What can you do today, even in your weakness, to step out in faith for Christ? Remember this important truth from *Philippians 4:13, "I can do everything through Christ who strengthens me."*

Don't limit God

"When we listen to men planning and arguing and thinking aloud, we get the impression of a vast number of things in this world which are known to be desirable but dismissed as impossible. Men spend the greater part of their lives putting limitations on the power of God. Faith is the ability to lay hold on that grace which is sufficient for all things in such a way that the things which are humanly impossible become divinely possible. With God all things are possible, and, therefore, the word impossible has no place in the vocabulary of the Christian and of the Christian Church." ~William Barclay

We limit God by a lack of faith and belief, fear and pride. *Psalm 147:5, "Great is our Lord and mighty in power; His understanding has no limit."* We limit God by not believing Him for His promises. God's word tells us that He is mighty and has no limit. Why then, do we limit God in our heads and hearts? When God puts a dream or a plan in a believer's heart, He puts the storehouses of heaven at our disposal to accomplish its purposes. We just need to believe it to receive it. If God has a plan, He will put the money, people and organizations in place to make it happen.

Ephesians 3:20 (MSG), "God can do anything, you know—far more than you could ever imagine or guess or request in your wildest dreams! He does it not by pushing us around but by working within us, His Spirit deeply and gently within us." Andrew Murray understood this when he said, "Faith expects from God what is beyond all expectation."

Mark 6:1-6 shows us that a lack of faith will hold back the power of God. "$_1$ Jesus left there and went to His hometown, accompanied by his disciples. $_2$ When the Sabbath came, He began to teach in

the synagogue, and many who heard Him were amazed."

"Where did this man get these things?" they asked. "What's this wisdom that has been given Him? What are these remarkable miracles He is performing? ₃ Isn't this the carpenter? Isn't this Mary's son and the brother of James, Joseph,[a] Judas and Simon? Aren't His sisters here with us?" And they took offense at Him.

₄ Jesus said to them, "A prophet is not without honor except in his own town, among his relatives and in his own home." ₅ **He could not do any miracles there ,except lay His hands on a few sick people and heal them 6 .He was amazed at their lack of faith..".**

Jesus could not do as many miracles there because of their lack of faith. The word reminds us in *2 Corinthians 5:7, "For we live by faith, not by sight."* The people were limited by what they could see and understand. If they couldn't understand it, it mustn't be possible. God doesn't want us to trust only what we can see in this world, He wants us to trust Him by faith for things much bigger than what we can see.

We can also limit God by fear. God does His work through His people. If you don't step up to the plate, He will do it through someone else and you will miss the blessing. Just because we can't do something in our own strength doesn't mean we couldn't do it in God's strength. God loves to show us what we can do through His power. We just need to trust Him.

God's plans will always take us out of our comfort zone because He wants us to need Him the whole way. If He gave us a plan that we were fully comfortable with to do on our own, we wouldn't seek His wisdom and we would think we didn't need Him. Truthfully, if it's not a bit scary, it's probably not God's plan for your life. This life is meant to stretch us further than we ever imagined.

One of the ways to battle fear is to trust God, one step at a time, one day at a time. Try to remove the word "overwhelmed" from your vocabulary. "When eating an elephant take one bite at a time." ~ Creighton Abrams. Ask God to show you what He needs you to do today. Allow God to help break your work down into manageable steps. Then, write those steps on a list and do them one at a time. Crossing off items from your list is empowering. Remember to celebrate accomplishments each day, too. Look at that partially eaten elephant and pat yourself on the back.

Probably the biggest culprit for limiting God is pride. Our sinful nature thinks we can do things by ourselves and asking for help is a sign of weakness. I'm sure you know someone who would rather drive around for hours than ask for directions. Humility is one of the most essential postures for being useable by God. We all have to work on peeling away those layers of pride to surrender to God's perfect will for us.

There is always a price to pay when we limit God. Regrets, disappointments and dissatisfaction in life are all symptoms of limiting God. I often wonder what it would be like to see a film showing what our lives would've been like if we fully trusted God's plans. We would probably be stunned by the missed opportunity and impact waiting for us. Perhaps, each of us could have impact like Billy Graham, Josh McDowell and Angus Buchan if we only trust God day-by-day for His sovereign guidance. These men have lived lives that seem like rare exceptions, but impact like theirs may be planned for every Christian. We may not know what we're missing this side of heaven, but as long as we draw breath, we can still make it better. God's power is released to faithful people. *Matthew 13: 12, "Whoever has will be given more, and they will have an abundance. Whoever does not have, even what they have will be taken from them."* When we limit God, we limit our own blessings.

Prepare your Fields: Clip from Facing the Giants

Do you ever feel impatient with God? You think you are doing what you're supposed to but things aren't happening fast enough for you? I know I feel that way from time to time. Maybe you can relate to coach Taylor in this clip from *Facing the Giants.*

Facing the Giants

http://bit.ly/12Jcmf5 [38]

PattySadallah.com Other Books tab Paperback Film Links, Facing the Giants

There are so many wonderful spiritual nuggets in this short clip. We'll look at the issues of waiting on the Lord, how to know when you should bloom where you are planted and preparing your fields to receive His blessings.

Coach Taylor had six failing years as a high school football coach when the community and parents were calling for his resignation. He was feeling like a failure and wanted to get out of this situation. But God used this humbling experience to prepare Him for a spiritual harvest at the high school when he put God at the center of his life.

Mr. Bridges quoted *Revelation 3:8, "I know your deeds. See, I have placed before you an open door that no one can shut. I know that you have little strength, yet you have kept my word and have not denied my name."* God alone opens and shuts the doors of opportunity in our lives. Our human nature causes us to want things to happen fast or to escape unpleasant experiences. God sees the entire plan. He knows how things will turn out in the end. There are plenty of reasons that God might ask us to wait. Sometimes we need to be ready for blessings. We may need to be spiritually mature enough to receive them or we will miss the point or take credit for God's work. God may need to prepare and orchestrate other people or organizations to be ready to partner with us in His grand plan. Sometimes 20/20 hindsight reveals His reasons for delays. In other cases, we may not know His reasons until we meet him in Heaven.

I Corinthians 7:17" Nevertheless, each person should live as a believer in whatever situation the Lord has assigned to them, just as God has called them." God often gives us glimpses of what He wants us to move toward, but we need to stay behind God. We may need education, more experience or humbling to be truly ready to step into that future. God will open the doors as you are ready. Meanwhile, trust Him every day to show you what you need to do to be ready for that future. If He wants you to be a missionary in Ecuador someday, He may provide a short-term missions trip or a language class to take while you keep your present job. Taking our own steps in the direction of a dream God has given us ahead of God's direction serves to slow down the process, not speed it up. We need to stay in the Word and in prayer so when He tells us to move, we can move with absolute assurance that every step is in His perfect will. And you can have direct confirmation from God through dialogue journaling conversations.

Waiting is never a pleasant experience, but we can be encouraged by this verse in *Isaiah 40:29-31 (NLT)*

"$_{29}$ He gives power to the weak

and strength to the powerless.

$_{30}$ Even youths will become weak and tired,

and young men will fall in exhaustion.

$_{31}$ But those who trust in the Lord will find new strength.

They will soar high on wings like eagles.

They will run and not grow weary.

They will walk and not faint."

Those who trust in the Lord will find the strength to wait. In our own flesh, we are weak, powerless and exhausted. But we get His strength when we trust in the Lord. Coach Taylor is like many of us. He prayed for something to happen and when it didn't happen fast enough, he was prepared to take matters into his own hands. But God hadn't told him it was time to leave his job.

God wants us to trust Him one day at a time. He demonstrated this with the Israelites in the wilderness with the pillars of fire and cloud. *Exodus 13:21, "By day the Lord went ahead of them in a pillar of cloud to guide them on their way and by night in a pillar of fire to give them light, so that they could travel by day or night."* The Lord went ahead of them. He guided their way one day at a time. When the pillars moved, they would break camp and move. But as long as the pillars stayed in their place, they would stay.

Nehemiah 9:19, "Because of your great compassion you did not abandon them in the wilderness. By day the pillar of cloud did not fail to guide them on their path, nor the pillar of fire by night to shine on the way they were to take." The Lord's guidance never fails. God wants to lead us day by day according to His will. Even if we don't see what He's up to, we need to trust Him because He is all knowing and sovereign.

Mr. Bridges told Coach Taylor a story about two farmers. Both farmers prayed for rain, but only one of the farmers prepared the field to receive it. Preparing the field is taking a step of faith. It's showing God that you believe His promises. That's what Angus Buchan did when he prayed for his potato crop in the middle of a drought. He had his hired hands prepared for a long season of harvest. He was the only farmer in that small town that trusted that there would be a crop at all. Most had let their workers go months before and didn't plant a crop.

Your step of faith may look like buying a new suit because you anticipate having the job God told you He would give you; or maybe you finally take steps to incorporate that nonprofit God has laid on your heart. Taking a step in the direction of God's calling shows that you mean business and you trust Him to keep His promises. When you have assurance in your heart about what God wants you to do, step out in faith.

There are lessons to learn in every circumstance. God is preparing you for the future He has planned for you. Continue to seek His guidance and direction and He will direct your path.

The Potter and His Clay: Clip from Surf's Up

"The board is already inside there somewhere, and what you are doing is you are trying to find it," Big Z told Cody while trying to teach him how to make a surfboard from a single piece of wood in this clip from *Surf's Up*. Cody was so impatient with his training. He's just like you and me, isn't he?

http://bit.ly/2UTqCnb [39]

See PattySadallah.com Other Books tab Paperback Film Links, Surf's Up

Even though Big Z had more experience, wisdom and knowledge, Cody, wanted to do things his own way. Cody didn't want Big Z's help. He just wanted to make his board by himself without the guidance of the master. Can you see how frustrated Big Z was at Cody's impatience, clumsiness and lack of finesse with the board? Sometimes I imagine God slapping His forehead at some of the stupid and prideful things that I do.

Without contact with the potter, the clay is nothing.

Just like that plank of wood, we start off as unrecognizable clay blobs of human shortcomings. We tend to muddle through life blind, full of issues and pride, creating messes all around us. We are all works in progress.

God wants to lead us toward being the best representation of ourselves that we can be, but we don't want to learn those lessons. We want to get to the destination without the hard work of the journey. CS Lewis said it best, "It may be hard for an egg to turn into a bird: it would be a jolly sight harder for it to learn to fly while remaining an egg. We are like eggs at present. And you cannot go on indefinitely being just an ordinary, decent egg. We must be hatched or go bad."

> "Isaiah 64:8, "Yet, O Lord, you are our Father. We are the clay, you are the potter; we are all the work of your hand."

When we stay in contact with the potter, the Living God, we can begin to change. Have you ever been really late and the traffic lights just worked in your favor? Or you find a ridiculously close parking space that saved you from being late for your meeting? How about that time you didn't get the job or the house that you thought you wanted and then God gave you a better one a bit later? Think about the people who missed work on 9/11 at the World Trade Center because they had the flu or were attending a funeral. God is sovereign.

No problem or challenge is too complicated for a sovereign Lord! Have you seen God take care of something right before your eyes this week? If you don't think He has been handling some crazy issues in your life, you just aren't paying attention or giving Him the credit. Pray that God would reveal to you more when He is working things out for you.

The Lord molds us to be beautiful. When we accept Christ and walk with Him daily, He begins to mold us into a new and more beautiful you and me. We become an improved version of ourselves, molded in His image. "The more we let God take us over, the more truly ourselves we become because He made us. He invented us. He invented all the different people that you and I were intended to be . . . It is when I turn to Christ, when I give up myself to His personality that I first begin to have a real personality of my own." ~ CS Lewis

Before we can embrace God's big plans, He needs to do some work on our character. We need to be ready to represent Him well. The more we work on our relationship with Christ the more we will become like Him and the more prepared we will be for what He has planned.

The Lord molds us to be useful. *2 Corinthians 4:7* says, *"We have this treasure from God, but we are like clay jars that hold the treasure."* God wants to develop us into kingdom-builders, useful and powerful. The very same power that raised Christ from the dead resides in the heart of every believer. God equips each of us for our own ministry of impact if we are pliable enough to allow Him to use us.

Psalm 139: 13-16 (MSG)

$^{13-16}$ Oh yes, you shaped me first inside, then out; you formed me in my mother's womb.

I thank you, High God—you're breathtaking!

Body and soul, I am marvelously made!

I worship in adoration—what a creation!

You know me inside and out, you know every bone in my body; You know exactly how I was made, bit by bit, how I was sculpted from nothing into something."

Just like the plank of wood being turned into a beautiful and useful surf board, God wants you to become what is already inside of you; you just need to find it. God wants to transform you into something beautiful and useful. How will you allow the potter to shape you today?

Spiritual Gifts and Finding Your Calling

God has assigned a calling for each and every believer. Your calling is not your job, although your job may be part of your calling. Finding your calling is related to finding the will of God for your life. At the core, that will is found in a clear understanding of your identity in Him. When you understand who you are and what God's will is, your experiences, passions, aptitudes and your spiritual gifts line up. Then God makes things happen and you find yourself in the flow of the Holy Spirit at the center of your calling.

The goal from God's perspective is not for you to do things for Him. But, for you to become the best version of yourself.

Your Christ-I will accomplish more for God when your focus is less about doing for Him and more about being with Him.

In the West and South chapters, we covered how overcoming life's challenges and sharing your faith with others can give you slingshot faith. Using those experiences to give hope and shed light on the path to victory for others blesses people. They may be significant to finding your calling. If you have been freed from an addiction or stronghold, God may want you to help others find their way to victory as well. A person that was saved by the efforts of a missionary may be inspired to reach other people in the same way.

Everyone has a guiding value, one that acts as the rudder to your ship. It helps you to see the world and creates boundaries for your life. If holiness is your guiding value, it will affect your decisions about what you watch on TV and what activities you will feel comfortable attending. If integrity is your guiding value, you will keep your promises and only do business with people and companies that you know to be honest and trustworthy.

Some values are umbrellas – they cover many things. I worked with a nonprofit once whose guiding value was citizenship. A good citizen would be law-abiding, respectful of others and property, and contributes positively to society. There are lots of values rolled up into one. Another example may be fruit-bearing. In order to bear fruit as a Christian, you must grow and develop your faith, and be willing to surrender and obey God's plan for the greatest impact.

Passions can be broken into two camps. We can have passions about doing certain things and we can have passions for serving people. To find your calling, explore both. Some people are drawn to certain populations. It may be because of their personality or their past experience. You may love to work with the elderly because you had a special relationship with a grandparent growing up. Or, you may love children because you are a fun-loving person and find joy in seeing the world through the eyes of children.

God can also break your heart for a certain population. You may have visited orphans in a third world country and it sparked a passion to help them. Or you lived through a natural disaster and appreciated the people who helped you and want to give back. You may find healing by helping people living with injustice because you lived through a tough experience and God brought you healing.

We can also be passionate because we have great skill or aptitude at something that brings us joy. Talents are God-given abilities to do things that come naturally to us. Writing, singing, playing instruments, organizing and speaking are skills to rely on, but when you add a love and passion for them, then they may be part of your calling.

Three types of Gifts

Every believer is given gifts by the Holy Spirit. Paul explains this in *1 Corinthians 12:4-6, "There are different kinds of gifts, but the same Spirit distributes them. $_5$ There are different kinds of service, but the same Lord. $_6$ There are different kinds of working, but in all of them and in everyone it is the same God at work."*

There are many gifts of the spirit. We will talk about what they are, and then we will talk how you may find yours. Biblical scholars have sorted these spiritual gifts into three categories; motivational gifts, ministry gifts, and manifestation gifts. Let's look at each of these categories, one at a time. There are plenty of free Spiritual Gifts assessments on the web if you want to know which gifts you possess. As you read the various gifts below, I recommend that you star the ones with which you most identify. This will help you later in the chapter when you do the *Finding your Calling Worksheet*.

Manifestation Gifts

Manifestation gifts are those that reveal the supernatural power of God. This category of gifts is the only one that is ours because of Jesus's finished work on the cross. Before Christ's redemptive work, the Holy Spirit would come upon prophets as He still does in the ministerial and motivational gifts that we will learn about in a bit. When the Holy Spirit entered your heart at the point of salvation, He came with nine gifts in tow. The Lord explained to me that they were like nine closed but unlocked doors in your heart. Every new covenant believer has all nine of these gifts behind the doors of their heart. We need to cooperate with God to release these gifts. It is sad that many believers will allow the Holy Spirit and these gifts to remain dormant in their lives for lack of awareness of this truth.

The Holy Spirit is in your heart in fullness. This prayer in *Ephesians 3:16-21* sheds light on the nature of these gifts:

> [16] *I pray that out of his glorious riches he may* **strengthen you with power through his Spirit in your inner being,** [17] *so that Christ may dwell in your hearts through faith. And I pray*

> that you, **being rooted and established in love,** ¹⁸ **may have power**, together with all the Lord's holy people, to grasp how wide and long and high and deep is the love of Christ, ¹⁹ and to know this love that surpasses knowledge—**that you may be filled to the measure of all the fullness of God.**
>
> ²⁰ Now to Him who is able to do immeasurably more than all we ask or imagine, **according to His power that is at work within us,** ²¹ to Him be glory in the church and in Christ Jesus throughout all generations, for ever and ever! Amen.

There is a direct correlation between the exercising of these gifts and your intimacy with Jesus. The more you focus your eyes on Jesus, spend time with Him in the Word, in prayer, worship and in encountering experiences, the more you are transformed into His likeness. This leads to an increased spiritual maturity that readies you to exercise more of these manifestation spiritual gifts.

All these gifts are yours as a born-again believer in Christ. Still, we are to desire the Gift-Giver over these gifts. Do not desire the gift of healing over the gift of the Holy Spirit's presence in your life. And never exercise one of these gifts out of your own personal pride or motivation, but only the prompting of the Holy Spirit.

All of the manifestation gifts of the Holy Spirit are supernatural, exercising power that is not limited to the natural laws of this world. The nine gifts are categorized by three of the mind, three of the mouth and three of the hands.

Mind

- **Word of Wisdom-** The ability to understand Scripture and have correct insight into its meaning. This can only come from the Holy Spirit giving you this insight. You cannot understand scripture properly with your head. The Holy Spirit lives in the heart, not the head. Solomon prayed for wisdom and God was pleased with him. He became the wisest man that ever lived. *1Kings 4:29, "God gave Solomon wisdom and very great insight, and a breadth of understanding as measureless as the sand on the seashore."*

- **Word of Knowledge-** The ability to remember and recall Biblical facts for the purpose of applying doctrinal truths to the body of Christ. It is also manifested by knowing something about a person that you couldn't possibly know apart from the Holy Spirit. Jesus demonstrated this gift when He spoke to the woman at the well about her past. See *John 4*.

- **Discernment-** The supernatural ability to discern good from evil and truth from lies. The gift of discernment is critical in checking the accuracy of a prophecy and knowing if a teaching from the pulpit or in a book is accurate or simply coming from a human perspective.

Mouth

- **Speaking in Tongues-** This is the ability to speak unknown languages. Primarily, this gift allows you to speak the heart of the Holy Spirit. It is a gift that blesses the receiver more than the body of Christ. Without the interpretation of tongues, the gift of tongues is a personal experience between the Holy Spirit and the tongue speaking person. Praying in tongues is praying God's perfect prayers of blessing for you and of worship to God. The teaching that warns to not speak in tongues without an interpreter is often taught incorrectly to suggest that this gift should not be used at all without an interpreter. This verse clearly dispels that teaching: *"If anyone speaks in a tongue, let there be two or at the most three, each in turn, and let one interpret. But if there is no interpreter, let him keep silent **in church**, and **let him speak to himself and to God**."* (1 Corinthians 14: 27-28) The warning is only for those who are not prompted by the Holy Spirit to speak tongues in public settings.

- **Interpretation of Tongues-** This gift is the supernatural ability to interpret the language of tongues. This gift is to be used in a public setting or if a person that speaks this language is in earshot of it and the Holy Spirit has a message to share with these audiences. Someone with this gift is able to bless the entire body of Christ by interpreting the message of the Holy Spirit by someone who just spoke in tongues.

- **Prophecy-** The closer this person is to God, the more insight God will give for you to share with others. It is important to note that all prophetic words need to match up with Scripture. God will never give a brand-new message, that is a message not consistent with His character, nature or Word. He will give a scripturally true message in a fresh way. I asked the Lord once to teach me about abiding and He gave me electricity as a metaphor. He showed me an unplugged toaster and said

"See that toaster? Unplugged it has no ability to serve as it was created to do. Plugged in, it is fully capable of behaving according to its true purpose." So, if someone tells you they got a message from God, and it doesn't line up with Scripture, it is not a message from God. Beware of false teachers.

Hands

- **Faith-** The gift of faith is not to be confused with the faith required for salvation. This in an activation gift. It demonstrates with action that you believe God. This is a supernatural faith given by the Holy Spirit to believe God for His promises and for miracles. I believed this gift was pivotal when I challenged a group of 40 people to a 30-day Faith Challenge. My hypothesis was that if you prayed for an increase in the gift of faith, you would see an increase in the manifestation of the other Holy Spirit gifts. That hypothesis bore true and the results of it will be in my <u>How to Find your Calling: Just ask Jesus Series Book 2</u> coming in 2019.

- **Healing-** People who exercise the gift of healing can effectively pray for healing by the mighty power of the Holy Spirit and see results that are beyond natural means. When someone with this gift lays hands on someone and they are healed, it is not the gifted person that accomplished the healing, it was the Holy Spirit working through that person.

   It is important to note that ALL believers are called to pray for healing by the authority of the Holy Spirit.

Those who exercise this gift have developed a faithful expectancy that the Lord will show up as the Great Physician and Healer with great power and effect. One of the most important lessons that I learned about healing is that God always desires perfect healing for everyone and that there is always a condition for every healing. Conditions can be physical, emotional, mental or spiritual.

- **Miracles-** Things that would seem impossible to man are possible with God. (See *Matthew 9:26*) You can live a life surrounded by miracles when you believe God to be who He says He is and live a life of expectancy that He will show up in all circumstances. The cool thing about the gift of miracles is that when you see God manifest Himself by signs, wonders and miracles, you expect to see it happen again and again. He loves to show Himself as His true limitless nature! As we have already shared in many stories in this book, miracles are happening in our time, just as they did in Jesus's day.

Ministry Gifts

Ministry Gifts are the tools that God gives people to do specific roles and build up the body of Christ. These are practical, role-driven capabilities that can overlap some of the other gift areas. These roles should not be limited to the walls of a church; you can live them out in everyday life. *Ephesians 4:11-13, "So Christ Himself gave the apostles, the prophets, the evangelists, the pastors and teachers, 12 to equip His people for works of service, so that the body of Christ may be built up 13 until we all reach unity in the faith and in the knowledge of the Son of God and become mature, attaining to the whole measure of the fullness of Christ."*

Every role needs to be played totally surrendered to the Holy Spirit for it to have kingdom impact. The Holy Spirit is in you and therefore He is with you regardless of what you are doing day to day. The hats you wear can change moment to moment and day to day depending on what you're doing at the time. Be aware that every moment of your time belongs to God.

- **Apostles/Missionaries-** This is a leadership gifting. Pastors as we think of them fall into this category because they need to lead for gifting in all categories. The original Apostles walked with Jesus. This is because the word apostle means foundation. Apostles are messengers for the foundation of the faith. People with this gift tend to plant churches and minister to other cultures. They are driven to carry out the Great Commission, God's directive to share the good news of Jesus Christ to the ends of the world. See *Ephesians 3:6-8* They look out for the spiritual welfare of others. They lead and direct the members of the church and see to it that they accomplish the purposes of the church. They motivate others to work in unity toward God's plans. As a parent in a family or a leader in your community or at work, you're also exercising the role of apostle.

- **Prophets-** As mentioned above, prophets speak God's word boldly and fearlessly. They are able to communicate divine truth and have a heart for the God's Word and message. They have the ability to speak the Truth in love. Whenever God gives you an opportunity to say something that will edify, uplift or bless someone, you are exercising this gift.

- **Evangelists-** People with this gift share the good news of salvation clearly and help lead people to Christ effectively and enthusiastically. They have a heart for the soul harvest. They build up the body of Christ by adding new members to its fellowship. Whenever you encourage, support or pray for God's best for someone, you are exercising this gift. You may have such opportunities in your family, work or community settings. Surrender those situations to the Lord and speak life whenever possible.

- **Pastors/Shepherds-** Those with this gift are responsible for protecting, guiding and caring for people. Essentially this is a helping role. Caring for the needs of the poor, your own family, and stepping in to meet basic needs are all examples of exercising this gift. Our western culture use of the title Pastor is more accurately an Apostle. Although Pastors serve the needs of their congregations in this capacity as well, their job is much broader than this biblical meaning entails.

- **Teachers-** This gift is about making sure people understand the Truth. Jesus said "I am the Way, the Truth, and the Tife". The truth is not a thing to know, it's a Person to know. This gift is exercised when someone helps you understand how to connect with God and make scripture clear. Parents ultimately have the great responsibility to play this role for their children. Bible study leaders are examples of exercising this gift.

- **Worship-** Worship leaders are gifted at singing and playing instruments in order to honor God. They are to use their gifts for edification more than for entertainment purposes. King David was a harp player and wrote many of the Psalms which are songs to the Lord. He valued music as a way to honor God. *2 Samuel 6:5, "David and all Israel were celebrating with all their might before the Lord, with castanets, harps, lyres, timbrels, sistrums and cymbals."* The role of worship is so much bigger than music and instruments. It also includes intercessory prayer, and simply soaking in God's Presence. When you connect with God in your quiet time or meet with Him in your special place, you are practicing the gift of worship.

- **Craftsmanship/Arts-** People with this gift can express the beauty of God and His creation using their hands. This gift is used to help people understand and relate to God, to honor and edify Him. Bezalel was the most mentioned craftsman in the Bible. *Exodus 36:1, "So Bezalel, Oholiab and every skilled person to whom the Lord has given skill and ability to know how to carry out all the work of constructing the sanctuary are to do the work just as the Lord has commanded."* All aspects of the arts are included in this gift. Pictures, stories, music and expressing emotions are all qualities of the language of the heart. This is God's language.

Motivational Gifts

Metaphorically speaking, when you become a believer, God gives you a primary filter or a lens through which to view the world. He will give you one of seven motivational gifts to use as your primary filter. As you go through life, you use this gift as a way to shape how you relate to people and impact the body of Christ. Even though you may have talents or interests in other areas, you're primarily filtering your heart motivations through one of these gifts. Essentially, God is connecting with you, showing you His heart through this lens more often than others.

- **Prophecy-** God will show you the hearts of people so you can help them to connect with God personally. He will give you the words that will enlighten, uplift and encourage them and draw them closer to God. See *Romans 12:6; 1 Corinthians 12:10*

- **Service/Helps/Hospitality-** God will help you recognize practical needs in the body of Christ so you may offer assistance in meeting those needs. This is the person who sees the homeless person on the street and stops to give them a hand, or notices the man struggling to lift his grocery bags to his trunk, drops what he is doing and runs to the rescue. People with this filter tend to do whatever it takes to help anyone in need. See *Romans 12:7, 1Peter 4:9-10*

- **Teaching-** This is the person whose heart burns for helping people understand God's Word and His ways. I can relate to this one. If I learn something that draws me closer to God, I can't help but share it. God allows these people to make complicated things easy to understand in order to help people understand, build up, unify and mature in the body of Christ. See *1 Corinthians 12:28, Romans 12:7, Ephesians 4:11*

- **Exhortation/Encouragement-** This is the person who senses that a person needs a hug, or a shoulder to cry on. They come alongside other believers with encouragement, comfort, consolation, and counsel to help them grow in their faith and grow to be all that God intends them to be. People with this gift are motivators of the faith and God gives them the exact words for each circumstance that will help them feel better. See *Romans 12:8*

- **Giving-** People with this filter serve with selfless generosity, a willingness to share all material resources they have liberally and joyfully without the thought of return. These people are supporters of God's agenda. See *Romans 12:8*

- **Administration/Organizing-** People with this gifting filter see when a group needs structure or a leader and step in to offer help. The ability to lead and steer the body of Christ toward the accomplishment of God-given goals by planning, organizing and supervising others. They can keep people on task and move them toward long-term goals. See *1Corinthians 12:28*

- **Mercy-** Those with this gifting cheerfully care for the needs of people, empathizing and giving help to those in need. People with this gift advocate and serve with love to help alleviate pain and distress. See *Romans 12:8*

These gifts are explained by scriptures below:

> *Romans 12:6-8, "$_6$ We have different gifts, according to the grace given to each of us. If your gift is prophesying, then prophesy in accordance with your[a] faith; $_7$ if it is serving, then serve; if it is teaching, then teach; $_8$ if it is to encourage, then*

give encouragement; if it is giving, then give generously; if it is to lead, [b] do it diligently; if it is to show mercy, do it cheerfully."

1 Corinthians 12:10-28, "$_{10}$ to another miraculous powers, to another prophecy, to another distinguishing between spirits, to another speaking in different kinds of tongues,[a] and to still another the interpretation of tongues.[b] $_{11}$ All these are the work of one and the same Spirit, and He distributes them to each one, just as He determines.

$_{12}$ Just as a body, though one, has many parts, but all its many parts form one body, so it is with Christ. $_{13}$ For we were all baptized by[c] one Spirit so as to form one body—whether Jews or Gentiles, slave or free—and we were all given the one Spirit to drink. $_{14}$ Even so the body is not made up of one part but of many.

$_{15}$ Now if the foot should say, "Because I am not a hand, I do not belong to the body," it would not for that reason stop being part of the body. $_{16}$ And if the ear should say, "Because I am not an eye, I do not belong to the body," it would not for that reason stop being part of the body. $_{17}$ If the whole body were an eye, where would the sense of hearing be? If the whole body were an ear, where would the sense of smell be? 18 But in fact God has placed the parts in the body, every one of them, just as He wanted them to be. $_{19}$ If they were all one part, where would the body be? $_{20}$ As it is, there are many parts, but one body.

> ₂₁ The eye cannot say to the hand, "I don't need you!" And the head cannot say to the feet, "I don't need you!" ₂₂ On the contrary, those parts of the body that seem to be weaker are indispensable, ₂₃ and the parts that we think are less honorable we treat with special honor. And the parts that are unpresentable are treated with special modesty, ₂₄ while our presentable parts need no special treatment. But God has put the body together, giving greater honor to the parts that lacked it, ₂₅ so that there should be no division in the body, but that its parts should have equal concern for each other. ₂₆ If one part suffers, every part suffers with it; if one part is honored, every part rejoices with it.
>
> ₂₇ Now you are the body of Christ, and each one of you is a part of it. ₂₈ And God has placed in the church first of all apostles, second prophets, third teachers, then miracles, then gifts of healing, of helping, of guidance, and of different kinds of tongues."

Let's try to make this personal. Before we get into the Finding your Calling Exercise that pulls together all the pieces of your calling, there's some pre-work we need to do to be ready to hear God's direction in this area.

The most important thing to consider about this entire chapter is that it's all about Him and not you. Your beginning point must always be God. I used to help people with this worksheet on the next page by asking them what they were "passionate" about. Perhaps a better question is: who is My God and How has He created me to serve? I have learned that it's not about my passion. It's about His compassion. He will help you connect with His heart regarding the piece of the wonderful tapestry of the body of Christ and show you exactly where you fit into His grand plans. The more time you spend with God the more your passion lines up with God's. Surrender your passions in favor of His compassions and watch what He can do through you!

Whenever you have something big that you need to work through with God, it's important to pause for prayer and confession. Confession clears the fog so you can see God clearly. So before we go into this exercise, ask God about your calling. Take some time to Praise, Repent, Ask and Yield. Thank God that He has a perfect plan for you. Confess any known sin and ask God to reveal to you something about your mission and calling. When you feel ready, you can work through this exercise.

Take a piece of paper and recreate this chart. Prayerfully work through the questions and see where God leads you.

Find your Calling Worksheet				
How has my past prepared me?	**What is my guiding value?**	**Who does God want me to serve?**	**What should I do?**	**What is the desired Kingdom Impact?**
What's my story? How has my past affected who I am? What lessons have I learned that I can use to help others?	What is my core value that drives my decision making? Which ONE Motivational Gift does God use as your filter?	What people or groups do I have a passion to serve? What issues has God put on my heart?	What skills and natural abilities do I love to do? What Ministry Gifts match my abilities?	How would people benefit from what you can do for them? Which Manifestation Gifts has God revealed through you?
Putting together everything that you worked through in this exercise; what do you believe God's calling is for you?				

I hope this guide helped you better understand how God has wired you for His service and for the special plan He has for you. Pray that God will help you understand more about what His plan is for you. Next, we will address the future pans God has for you.

BHAGS

When we vacation in Florida, we have hours of driving through the mountains. The views are mesmerizing. I saw a wonderful house set high on the side of the mountain like it was cut into the rock. Those mountains and that house are like your future. God can give you a glimpse of something beautiful He has planned for you in the distance. But you can't see the roads, obstacles, dangers or terrain that it will take to get you there. God gives us a picture of the goal, but He doesn't give us the details of the journey.

Left to our own devices, we will always shoot lower than God's plan for us. The disciples lived with Jesus and they still had trouble understanding they were capable of more than they imagined. When Jesus casted out a demon that they failed to, they asked Him a question. *Matthew 17:19-20, "Then the disciples came to Jesus privately and said, 'Why could we not cast it out?' He said to them, 'Because of your little faith. For truly I tell you, if you have faith the size of a mustard seed, you will say to this mountain, 'Move from here to there,' and it will move; and nothing will be impossible for you.'"* We need to believe God for the plan that He has for us. Even when it is bigger than we think we can handle. It takes ever growing faith.

Luke 17:5-6, "The apostles said to the Lord, 'Increase our faith!' The Lord replied. 'If you had faith the size of a mustard seed, you could say to this mulberry tree, 'Be uprooted and planted in the sea,' and it would obey you.'" The Word above says that all it takes is faith the size of a mustard seed for miraculous results Did you catch that little dot? *That* is the size of a mustard seed. Did you know that mustard plants grow from a seed that size to a tree that can be as tall as 20 feet? Seems easy enough to have faith that size right? Truthfully, we can't even have faith the size of that little dot apart from God.

At the beginning of every year, our Truth at Work Christian Roundtable group would set Big Hairy Audacious God-sized goals (BHAGS). Those are goals given by God and are so big that we could never achieve them outside of His providence. I can tell you, these goals were doozies! We would pray and journal the goals that God would have us achieve in our personal, spiritual and vocational lives. Then we would think through what it would take for all of us to get there.

There was a man who God challenged to give away more money that year than he had ever earned. That's a BHAG! It took getting outside His comfort zone, hard work, daily surrender and faithful prayer but he accomplished that goal! He was able to flow money to ministries that he never thought he could afford to help that year. More important than the money was the spiritual growth that he enjoyed by trusting and obeying God enough to accomplish the goal.

Our impact is our promised land, so when God puts goals on our hearts that big, it's easy to be like the Israelites. Even after personally witnessing the awesome power of the Great I AM, they were still too afraid to enter the Promised Land because they saw a few giants. The secret to having faith is surrender. Letting God be God and getting out of His way so that He can make it happen. To accomplish God's plans we need to pray, surrender, listen and act.

Pray for increased faith and wisdom. Wisdom and faith are two of the spiritual gifts that you can ask for that God delights to give you. The more you believe God for His promises, the more your faith will rise, and you will walk in that belief. *Hebrews 11:6, "And without faith it is impossible to please God, because anyone who comes to Him must believe that He exists and that He rewards those who earnestly seek Him."*

Surrender the goal to God. BHAGS are bigger than we can accomplish by ourselves, so we'll need to lean on Him to accomplish them. God wants us to need Him. The way to show Him we're serious is to step out in faith and go for them. Remind yourself it's God's plan, not your own. If He's the omnipotent boss, His ways will be wiser than yours, so your best bet is to surrender to God.

Listen to His voice. No matter how big the goal God has put on your heart, He will fully equip you to accomplish it. *Ephesians 4:11-13 (NIV), "$_{11}$ So Christ Himself gave the apostles, the prophets, the evangelists, the pastors and teachers, $_{12}$ to equip His people for works of service, so that the body of Christ may be built up $_{13}$ until we all reach unity in the faith and in the knowledge of the Son of God and become mature, attaining to the whole measure of the fullness of Christ."*

Do what He asks one day at a time to accomplish the goal. I muddled through one learning curve after another, but God directed my steps one day at a time to get this book published. It was a year and a half after He gave me the initial book concept that He revealed the way to publish it in paperback. When I started this process, I had no idea what an enhanced book (one that includes media) or a QR code (used in the first version as the primary way to view the content) was and yet, God worked out every detail and brought along multiple ministry partners to accomplish the goal!

Future Vision

Here is a writing exercise that will help you get a glimpse from God about what He has planned for you and what your goals may be. This is the same process that we worked through with the roundtable group mentioned above.

Begin with a significant time of prayer. If finding your calling and God's plan is important to you, I would recommend fasting and praying before you enter into this exercise. Fasting is not necessary, but when used in conjunction with prayer, it positions you for a breakthrough. The denial of food or something else along with prayer provides spiritual cleansing that allows you to hear more clearly from God.

Fix your eyes on Jesus for this exercise. Bring Him into the scene. Doing this exercise apart from Him is a dead work.

Confession is another important step to preparing your heart to hear God's direction. Journal anything you need to confess and ask God to forgive you for these sins. This will give you a clean slate and also allow you to hear from God more clearly.

You'll need a pen and paper for this next step. It is a nonstop writing exercise for about 10 minutes. Writing nonstop is important because this exercise works best when you are using the creative side of your brain. If you 'think' too much, it will not work. Our own limiting thoughts will creep in and it won't be from God.

After preparing your heart and praying that God will use this opportunity to show you a glimpse of His plans and goals for you, you are ready for the writing exercise.

You will be writing a letter to someone who would be interested and supportive of your accomplishments. The letter will have a beginning, middle and end. Here are the steps of the exercise. You may want to print them so you can glance at them while you are doing the exercise but remember not to stop or pause along the way.

1. Date the letter today's date 1-5 years into the future. Don't date the letter further than 5 years because it's too difficult for us to grasp that far into the future. Five years is the typical time period, but it can be done in any increment from one to five.

2. Address the letter to anyone you feel would be interested and supportive of your future. You are writing about your ideal future day where you are serving God with your gifts and talents according to His perfect will. Like every day, your future day will have a beginning, middle and an end.

3. Beginning: Wake up and using all of your senses, notice what you see, smell, taste, touch and hear. This will awaken the creative side of your brain. Are you living in a new place? Driving a new car? What do you smell? Etc.

4. Middle: Next, you have your ideal day. What are you doing? How are you serving? Who are you serving? Who's with you? Where are you? Are there special technologies that you see helping you? A new place? New people? How do you *know* that you are having the impact that God would desire? What is satisfying about it?

5. Answer a question: Next, someone comes up to you and congratulates you on your amazing life and fruit-bearing impact. You thank them and they ask you, "What was the biggest thing that you had to overcome to get to this point?" You answer them.

6. End: To close the exercise, end your day with a celebration. You can celebrate any way you want, with anyone you want. This is just a fun way to close the exercise.

Once you finish journaling your exercise, pray for wisdom and discernment about what it means. Seek Godly counsel about what some of the steps to get there. I always warn people that the vision that God gives you may be scary. Remember, if it's not a bit scary, it's not from God. You may even want to reject the vision as you are journaling because it sounds too outrageously big for you to accomplish. Stick with it. God would not show you something that He would not equip you to carry out. Keep writing what God shows you and spend time in reflection about what God wants for you.

Don't quit your job the day you do this exercise. God may show you a new job, but He also may have some steps along the way before He moves you. Let Him tell you clearly what to do and when His timing is perfect.

Ephesians 2:10 reminds us, *"For we are God's handiwork, created in Christ Jesus to do good works, which God prepared in advance for us to do."* Dig into this, take it seriously, and God will give you clarity about your calling and the plans He has for you. His plans are always good!

Ideal Future Vision Exercise
Journal this letter using this guide for 10 minutes nonstop

Today's Date (1-5 years in the future)

Dear_____,

Beginning: Use all of your senses. Wake up. What do you see smell, taste, touch, feel?

Middle: Ideal Future: Write about the details that God shows you about what you are doing, for whom, and how you know it is blessing people

What did you have to overcome?

End with a celebration.

Life Application: EAST

1. What kind of legacy do you want to leave?

2. Reflecting on the *Work is Worship* clip and message; how can your work be a way to worship the Lord? Go to Biblegateway.com or your Bible concordance and search the word 'work.' Look up at least three scriptures you can find about work and apply them to your own work situation.

3. If God has put a clear direction on your heart, what can you do to step out in faith today?

4. In what ways do you limit God?

5. What was your biggest take away from the *Facing the Giants* clip and message?

6. What did you learn about yourself related to God from the Potter and his Clay section and the *Surf's Up* clip?

7. Work through the Finding Your Calling chart. What do you think God is preparing you for? What insights did you gain about your calling?

8. Do the BHAG writing assignment and reflect on the vision that God gave you about the future that He is planning for you.

BACK TO CENTER
Living the Abundant Christian Life

Let's summarize what we have been learning as we study the Territory of Christian Impact.

Begin Center- Choose Jesus

God is love. God created the world and everything in it just so He could have a relationship with people. He sent Jesus to be a perfect sacrifice for us. Jesus chooses you to be part of His adopted family. It's His will that all be saved. *1 Timothy 2:2-6,*

> *"I urge, then, first of all, that petitions, prayers, intercession and thanksgiving be made for all people— $_2$ for kings and all those in authority, that we may live peaceful and quiet lives in all godliness and holiness. $_3$ This is good, and pleases God our Savior, $_4$ who wants all people to be saved and to come to a knowledge of the truth. $_5$ For there is one God and one mediator between God and mankind, the man Christ Jesus, 6 who gave Himself as a ransom for all people. This has now been witnessed to at the proper time."*

God is alive and shows Himself through creation, intimate communication, dreams, visions, miracles and answered prayers and direct encounters. Reading the Word of God and prayer are primary ways that we can learn from and communicate with God daily. God desires to lead us one day at a time.

If you have not yet accepted Jesus, He is knocking on your heart right now. I know this because you are reading this book. When you receive Christ, the Holy Spirit takes up permanent residence in your heart. He gives you a spiritual gift that equips you to accomplish your calling. You are sealed in the name of Jesus Christ and you have an irrevocable ticket to Heaven. *Revelation 3:5, "The one who is victorious will, like them, be dressed in white. I will never blot out the name of that person from the book of life but will acknowledge that name before my Father and His angels."*

North- Grow your relationship with Christ

Once you have accepted Christ, you grow your relationship with God by spending time getting to know His character and Truth. Developing holy habits of reading the word of God, praying according to the promises in the Bible and most importantly, spending time encountering God directly make Him real to you. God Is love and when you spend time with Him, His love brings power for mighty miracles, healing, freedom and healing.

West-Overcome life's challenges and find forgiveness

As you grow in your relationship with God, you become more like Christ. More gifts are revealed as you mature in faith. As you allow Jesus to transform you into His likeness, you are more able to forgive past hurts and overcome life's challenges because you have the Holy Spirit within you and you don't need to handle these things alone. You can enjoy the Fruit of the Spirit and you begin to have the attitudes and actions of Christ.

South-Leverage life's circumstances to share your faith and light

Just as people are put in your life to help you, God will allow you to share your light and faith through the people and circumstances He puts in your life. As you find victory, you will also find the courage to share your faith and help others. God has uniquely qualified you to do this.

East-Use your gifts to bless others and advance Kingdom plans

The Promised Land for believers today is to bear fruit and have kingdom impact. God desires to knit together believers as the collective body of Christ to accomplish His kingdom purposes. All of this leads to the abundant Christian life and more Fruit of the Spirit. When you find your calling, your true purpose in life, you will be effective and advance the kingdom.

Back to Center- Live the abundant Christian life

As you grow in each of the compass areas, the center circle grows as well because they are all connected. God is a God of multiplication, so like seeds that bear crops 100 times greater than planted, your heavenly reward will be multiplied. The more fruit you bear on earth, the exponentially more rewards you will have to enjoy for eternity.

Before we close, we will look at the issues of finishing well, your eternal rewards and ways you can shine your light.

How will you be remembered? Legacy Clip

http://bit.ly/2SHGk7j [40]

See PattySadallah.com Other Books tab Paperback Film Links, Legacy

This *Legacy* clip will make you think about how you will be remembered. Many Christians are like Frank; either they hide their faith, or they are bad representations of Christ. *Romans 3:15-16, "I know your deeds, that you are neither cold nor hot. I wish you were either one or the other! 16 So, because you are lukewarm—neither hot nor cold—I am about to spit you out of my mouth."*

Frank spent his days hiding his faith or misrepresenting it. Unfortunately, many Christians are known more for what they are against than what they are for. God wants us to make faith in Him attractive. Don't be like Frank. His lukewarm Christian life will have eternal consequences.

Jesus was highly offended by the self-righteous attitudes of the Pharisees. *Matthew 15:1-2, "Some Pharisees and teachers of* religious law now arrived from Jerusalem to see Jesus. They asked Him, 2 "Why do your disciples disobey our age-old tradition? For they ignore our tradition of ceremonial hand washing before they eat."

Jesus responded, Matthew 15:3-9,

> "Jesus replied, "And why do you, by your traditions, violate the direct commandments of God? But you say it is all right for people to say to their parents, 'Sorry, I can't help you. For I have vowed to give to God what I would have given to you.' $_6$ In this way, you say they don't need to honor their parents. [c] And so you cancel the word of God for the sake of your own tradition. $_7$ You hypocrites! Isaiah was right when he prophesied about you, for he wrote,
>
> $_8$ 'These people honor me with their lips,
>
> but their hearts are far from me.
>
> $_9$ Their worship is a farce, for they teach man-made ideas as commands from God.'[d]"

The Barna Group conducts research related to American worldviews and the Biblical understanding of the Christian worldview. It was interesting to learn that the number one reason Americans will say they accepted Christ was because of the actions or influence of another Christian. Unfortunately, the number one reason Americans will say they don't plan to accept Christ is also because of the actions or influence of another Christian.

Recently, the Barna Group examined the question "Are American Christians more like Jesus or more self-righteous like the Pharisees?"[41] A statistically representative sample of Christians was asked to respond to statements by rating their agreement on a four-point scale. They rated statements about self-righteous actions and attitudes and compared them to ratings of Christ-like actions and attitudes. The research statements used to examine Christ-likeness include the following:

Actions like Jesus:

- I listen to others to learn their story before telling them about my faith.
- In recent years, I have influenced multiple people to consider following Christ.
- I regularly choose to have meals with people with very different faith or morals from me.
- I try to discover the needs of non-Christians rather than waiting for them to come to me.
- I am personally spending time with non-believers to help them follow Jesus.

Attitudes like Jesus:

- I see God-given value in every person, regardless of their past or present condition.
- I believe God is for everyone.
- I see God working in people's lives, even when they are not following Him.
- It is more important to help people know God is for them than to make sure they know they are sinners.
- I feel compassion for people who are not following God and doing immoral things.

The statements used to assess self-righteousness (like the Pharisees), included the following research items:

Self-Righteous Actions:

- I tell others the most important thing in my life is following God's rules.
- I don't talk about my sins or struggles. That's between me and God.
- I try to avoid spending time with people who are openly gay or lesbian.
- I like to point out those who do not have the right theology or doctrine.
- I prefer to serve people who attend my church rather than those outside the church.

Self-Righteous Attitudes:

- I find it hard to be friends with people who seem to constantly do the wrong things.
- It's not my responsibility to help people who won't help themselves.
- I feel grateful to be a Christian when I see other people's failures and flaws.
- I believe we should stand against those who are opposed to Christian values.
- People who follow God's rules are better than those who do not.

The Findings:

Using these 20 questions as the basis of analysis, the researchers created an aggregate score for each individual and placed those results into one of four categories, or quadrants. The four categories and the results were:

- Christ-like in action and attitude- 14%
- Christ-like in action, but not in attitude- 14%
- Christ-like in attitude, but not action- 21%
- Christ-like in neither- 51%

That means that 72% of Christian Americans are misrepresenting the faith. I believe that God wants every believer to be in the first quadrant. If we all lived with Christ-like actions and attitudes it would change the world.

How we live speaks louder than what we say. Don't offend with your witness like Frank did when he went to jail for behaving violently at the abortion clinic. Christianity is a lifelong journey. No one will reach perfection, but we can all draw closer and live like Christ more and more each passing day. Finish well.

> *Deuteronomy 30:19 says, "Today I have given you the choice between life and death, between blessings and curses. Now I call on heaven and earth to witness the choice you make. Oh, that you would choose life, so that you and your descendants might live!"*
>
> *Joshua 24:15, "But if you refuse to serve the Lord, then choose today whom you will serve... But as for me and my family, we will serve the Lord."*

The Crowns: Eternal Rewards

The Crown of Life mentioned earlier is one of the eternal rewards that God promises to give the faithful believer, but it's not the only one. Before we talk about all of them, it is important to mention that salvation is not a reward. It is a gift from God to any believer who chooses to accept it. Once you have accepted Christ as your Savior, you are sealed until Jesus returns. *2 Timothy 2:19, "Nevertheless, God's solid foundation stands firm, sealed with this inscription: 'The Lord knows those who are His,' and, 'Everyone who confesses the name of the Lord must turn away from wickedness.'"* You cannot lose your ticket to heaven.

But your heavenly rewards are earned. They can be lessened or lost if you backslide, have bitterness in your heart, or simply keep your faith to yourself and fail to live the life that God has planned for you. *2 John 1:8 (AMP), "Look to yourselves (take care) that you may not lose (throw away or destroy) all that we and you have labored for, but that you may [persevere until you] win and receive back a perfect reward [in full]."* Notice that this verse is referring to your reward, not your salvation.

Not every believer that enters Heaven will receive a crown. These crowns are not like a trophy that you receive at a banquet and then put on a shelf or in a box in the attic. These are eternal rewards that impact you forever. And they are promised by Jesus. *Revelation 22:12 (AMP), "Behold, I am coming soon, and I shall bring My wages and rewards with Me, to repay and render to each one just what his own actions and his own work merit."*

The more fruit you bear in this life, the greater your reward will be in Heaven. It's not clear exactly what that means, but you may have a more brilliant heavenly body or clothing, *Daniel*

12:3 (MSG), "Men and women who have lived wisely and well will shine brilliantly, like the cloudless, star-strewn night skies. And those who put others on the right path to life will glow like stars forever." Some will have the honor of sharing the responsibility to rule and reign with Jesus.

The Territory of Christian Impact Model is key to understanding how eternal rewards work. As you grow your faith in the areas we covered in the North, West, South and East, you will grow your Abundant Christian Life in the Center. The more you grow that center, the better your eternal reward and experience will be in heaven.

The Crown of Life- This one is known as the Martyrs' Crown. This is for someone who patiently endures trials, testing and temptations. They are faithful even until death. *Revelation 2:10 (AMP), "Fear nothing that you are about to suffer. [Dismiss your dread and your fears!] Behold, the devil is indeed about to throw some of you into prison, that you may be tested and proved and critically appraised, and for ten days you will have affliction. Be loyally faithful unto death [even if you must die for it], and I will give you the crown of life."*

The Crown of Righteousness- Also known as the Victors Crown reserved for people who strive to live lives of Holiness. Their Christ-like service to people for God was met without selfish motives. They are ready for Christ's return. *2 Timothy 4:7-8 (AMP), "$_7$ I have fought the good (worthy, honorable, and noble) fight, I have finished the race, I have kept (firmly held) the faith. $_8$ [As to what remains] henceforth there is laid up for me the [victor's] crown of righteousness [for being right with God and doing right], which the Lord, the righteous Judge, will award* to me and recompense me on that [great] day—and not to me only, but also to all those who have loved and yearned for and welcomed His appearing (His return)."

The Crown of Rejoicing- This crown is given to those who contagiously express their faith and lead others to follow Christ. This one can also be known as the soul winner's crown. *1 Thessalonians 2:19, "For what is our hope, our joy, or the crown in which we will glory in the presence of our Lord Jesus when He comes..."*

The Incorruptible Crown- This is also known as the Imperishable Crown, reserved for those who find victory from strongholds, letting go of things of this life that take us away from God. These people have mastered putting God first in their lives. *1 Corinthians 9:24-27, "$_{24}$ Do you not know that in a race all the runners run, but only one gets the prize? Run in such a way as to get the prize. $_{25}$ Everyone who competes in the games goes into strict training. They do it to get a crown that will not last, but we do it to get a crown that will last forever. $_{26}$ Therefore I do not run like someone running aimlessly; I do not fight like a boxer beating the air. $_{27}$ No, I strike a blow to my body and make it my slave so that after I have preached to others, I myself will not be disqualified for the prize."*

The Crown of Glory- This one for leaders, pastors, shepherds of the flock; for people who invest in the growth of others in Christ. *1 Peter 5:2-5, "Be shepherds of God's flock that is under your care, watching over them—not because you must, but because you are willing, as God wants you to be; not pursuing dishonest gain, but eager to serve; $_3$ not lording it over those entrusted to you, but being examples to the flock. $_4$ And when the Chief Shepherd appears, you will receive the crown of glory that will never fade away."*

Live your life in a manner worthy of a crown reward. On Judgment Day, every believer should desire to hear God say as He did in *Matthew 25:21,* *"Well done, good and faithful servant! You have been faithful with a few things; I will put you in charge of many things. Come and share your master's happiness."*

Plant the Seed: Clip from *The Lorax*

The animated film *The Lorax* is set in the city of Thneedville, where everything is fake and even the air is manufactured because there are no trees. Ted has a crush on Audrey, whose dream is to see a real tree. On a mission to impress her, 12-year-old Ted seeks out the Onceler, the town founder who invented thneeds and cut down all of the town trees to produce them. Now living as a hermit outside of town, the Onceler shares his story of how his dream of helping the community with his company was stamped out by greed. Against the better advice and counsel of the wise Lorax, the Onceler devastated the land making way for the greedy Mayor to exploit the unhealthy environmental circumstance by selling man-made air.

In this clip, the Onceler confesses the whole story to Ted and inspires him to do something about it.

The Lorax

http://bit.ly/14EhvKL [42]

See PattySadallah.com Other Books tab Paperback Film Links, The Lorax

This is a wonderful film with spiritual wisdom peppered throughout. The Lorax character represents the Holy Spirit. He is the still small voice, our conscience that tells us right and wrong. In the beginning of the film, the Lorax comes alongside the Onc-ler as a friend, warning and guiding him along the way. The Onceler began his business journey with a desire to impress his hard-to-please family and to help the community with his thneed invention. The lack of trees caused a serious health risk to the townspeople but, the Onceler didn't concern himself with that reality. When greed overcame him, the Onceler pushed aside the Lorax completely and chopped down the very last tree.

The seed that the Onceler held onto represents the hope we have that all things can change, including ourselves. "It may seem small and insignificant. But, it's not about what it is, but what it can become." Onceler's words are true for both good and evil. He didn't realize at the time that he was sowing seeds of desolation with his greed. He was employing people in the town and they seemed happy with his thneeds. He thought he was the good guy. But greed took him down a road that he didn't anticipate.

Remember the message from the *Unconditional* clip? It's not a dead end if it takes you where you need to go. By sharing his mistakes and showing Ted the step he could take to help turn it around, the Onceler had his chance at redemption.

Why do you think the Onceler wanted the tree planted in the middle of town where everyone could see it? *Matthew 5:14* holds the answer, *"You are the light of the world. A town built on a hill cannot be hidden."* The seed was bigger than Ted. The tree needed to grow and multiply the center of town prominently placed to bless everybody. Ted needed to do something with the seed. He needed to have the courage to go against what was normal and do something that was right. He had the information and the power to choose to plant that seed in the center of town. If you get a chance to watch *The Lorax*, you'll see that it turned out well for the whole town.

I was thinking about the word "unless" carved into the rock at the beginning of the clip and I wondered what scripture had to say about that word. There were 60 verses with that word in the NIV alone. Let's take a look at a few of them in summary of what we have already learned in this book.

Unless...

Jesus knocks on the door of your heart

John 6:44, "No one can come to me unless the Father who sent me draws them, and I will raise them up at the last day."

John 6:65, "He went to say, "This is why I told you that no one can come to me unless the Father has enabled them."

You accept His free gift

*John 3:5, "Jesus answered, "Very truly I tell you, no one can enter the kingdom of God **unless** they are born of water and the Spirit."*

*Amos 3:3, "Do two walk together **unless** they have agreed to do so?"*

You let Him transform you

*Matthew 18:3, "And He said: 'Truly I tell you, **unless** you change and become like little children, you will never enter the kingdom of heaven.'"*

*John 12:24, "Very truly I tell you, **unless** a kernel of wheat falls to the ground and dies, it remains only a single seed. But if it dies, it produces many seeds."*

God helps us along the way

*Psalm 94:17, "**Unless** the Lord had given me help, I would soon have dwelt in the silence of death."*

*John 15:4, "Remain in me, as I also remain in you. No branch can bear fruit by itself; it must remain in the vine. Neither can you bear fruit **unless** you remain in me."*

*John 16:7, "But very truly I tell you, it is for your good that I am going away. **Unless** I go away, the Advocate will not come to you; but if I go, I will send*

Him to you."

You can help others find their way too

Romans 10:15, "And how can anyone preach **unless** they are sent? As it is written: 'How beautiful are the feet of those who bring good news!'"

Do Something

Matthew West has a song that speaks to this issue perfectly. Here is a lyric video of him singing "Do Something." I loved this song from the first time I heard it.

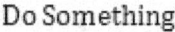

http://bit.ly/1aH879a [43]

See PattySadallah.com Other Books tab Paperback Film Links, Do Something

Shine Your Light Clip

Your relationship with God is your love story. This is what the Bible has to say about love:

1 Corinthians 13:1-13

"If I could speak all the languages of earth and of angels, but didn't love others, I would only be a noisy gong or a clanging cymbal. ² If I had the gift of prophecy, and if I understood all of God's secret plans and possessed all knowledge, and if I had such faith that I could move mountains, but didn't love others, I would be nothing. ³ If I gave everything I have to the poor and even sacrificed my body, I could boast about it; [a] but if I didn't love others, I would have gained nothing.

⁴ Love is patient and kind. Love is not jealous or boastful or proud ⁵ or rude. It does not demand its own way. It is not irritable, and it keeps no record of being wronged. ⁶ It does not rejoice about injustice but rejoices whenever the truth wins out. ⁷ Love never gives up, never loses faith, is always hopeful, and endures through every circumstance.

⁸ Prophecy and speaking in unknown languages[a] and special knowledge will become useless. But love will last forever! ⁹ Now our knowledge is partial and incomplete, and even the gift of prophecy reveals only part of the whole picture! ¹⁰ But when the time of perfection comes, these partial things will become useless.

¹¹ When I was a child, I spoke and thought and reasoned as a child. But when I grew up, I put away childish things. ¹² Now we see things imperfectly, like puzzling reflections in a mirror, but then we will see everything with perfect clarity. [a] All that I know now is partial and incomplete, but then I will know everything completely, just as God now knows me completely.

¹³ Three things will last forever—faith, hope, and love—and the greatest of these is love."

Since God is love and our ability to love comes from God, we need to stay close to Him so we can have His attitudes and allow them to become our behaviors. Love is not like a glass of water, limited in size by its container and reduced when poured. Love is like a candle, when one lights another, there is more light, not less. Check out this illustration video about *Your Light*.

Shine your Light

http://bit.ly/2N1uRub [44]

PattySadallah.com Other Books tab Paperback Film Links, Shine Your Light

Matthew 15:16, "In the same way, let your light shine before others, that they may see your good deeds and glorify your Father in heaven."

Life Application: Back to Center

1. Reflecting on the *Legacy* clip, what do you think people would say about you if you died today? Are your attitudes and behaviors more self-righteous or Christ-like?

2. Which Crowns do you think you will receive? What can you change to improve your legacy?

3. What was your biggest take-away from *The Lorax* clip and the Matthew West song?

4. What can you do to show Christ's love and shine your light?

About the Author

Patty Sadallah was saved at the age of 20 and is pleased to be able to serve the Lord with her gifts.

It is her passion and mission to help people grow in their love relationship and faith in Jesus and live out their callings so they may have tremendous Kingdom impact. She brings over 3 decades of experience as a nonprofit and faith-based organization development consultant, coach, facilitator, speaker and trainer.

Patty has a Doctorate of Ministry in Christian Leadership and Discipleship at Christian Leadership University and serves the University as a Professor and Leader of the Mentored Group Coaching Membership Program for it's School of the Spirit. She has a Masters of Organizational Development from American

University and Bachelors of Organizational Communication from Ohio University. She has served non-profit faith-based organizations in planning capacities for more than 35 years. She is a Master Facilitator and Disciple Maker, aiding individuals and organizations to connect with Jesus to find the road and plans that God has for them.

Clips that Move Mountains was her first book. *Journey to the Abundant Christian Life* is a Bible study companion to this book. *How to Life a Worry-Free Life* is the first of the *Just Ask Jesus* book series. Look for the next book in that series: *How to Find your Calling* coming in 2019.

Patty has been married to George since 1986 and they have three lovely daughters, Jamael who is married to Nick, Leah and Noelle. Jamael and Nick have given them two sweet granddaughters. George and Patty live in North Royalton, Ohio.

Contact her at *Patty@PattySadallah.com* if you would like to have her coach, speak or train at your church or organization or event.

Featured Filmmakers and Other Partners

Please check out this additional information about these supporting film companies and other partners that helped with this project.

- ❖ Global Creative Studios- Faith Like Potatoes

    www.FaithLikePotatoes.com

Frans Cronje, owner of Global Creative Studios, produced *Faith like Potatoes*. He has the life purpose to "tell stories that inspire", as his part in fulfilling the Great Commission. *Faith Like Potatoes* is about the inspiring true story of the early years of Angus Buchan's amazing life and faith. See more about their work in www.franscronje.tv.

- ❖ Echoing Praise- Prophetic Proof

    www.EchoingPraise.com

Identical twins, Misty and Kristy, "echo praises to God" through their dance and TV Ministry. Founders of EP Dance Studio and directors/teachers of an anointed ministering team. They also create and produce an hour-long, weekly TV show featuring worship, dance, music videos, interviews, preaching, and illustrations like included clip: "Prophetic Proof". Their powerful, inspiring videos touch hearts and change lives around the world! Additionally, they offer custom dance choreography and audio/video services to other ministries and songwriters. http://www.echoingpraise.com AND http://www.youtube.com/echoingpraise

- ❖ **Faith Street Film Partners- King's Faith**

    www.KingsFaith.com

KING'S FAITH is written, directed and produced by Nicholas DiBella of Faith Street Film Partners. After Brendan King's life spiraled to rock bottom, the teen found hope in a new relationship with Christ while serving time in a juvenile penitentiary. In his darkest moment, Brendan found faith. Now he must decide if it's worth the price to hold on to it. Available on DVD from Provident Films, *KING'S FAITH* stars Emmy Award winner Lynn Whitfield, along with Crawford Wilson, Kayla Compton, and James McDaniel. Get your copy of King's Faith and be inspired!

- ❖ **Floodgate Productions-God Speaks**

    www.FloodgateProductions.com

We tell great stories, using media. Floodgate Productions provides mini-movies, short motions and countdowns that help pastors and churches share the message of the gospel in a creative and impactful way. Visit their website and see you can enhance your messages with media.

- ❖ **James Grocho- Your Light Clip**

    www.JamesGrocho.com

James Grochowalski creates high quality mini sermons, countdowns, motions, and templates. He believes media is a necessary, fun, and helpful tool to bring people to Christ. He is happy to use his gifts & talents in a way that further the kingdom of God. Check out his other work at www.JamesGrocho.com

❖ **Christian Film Database- Film Resource Information Site**

www.ChristianFilmDatabase.com

Christian Film Database is a non-denominational online Christian Movie List and resource center all in one place, easy to find. CFDb desires to see Christians and non-Christians find films that will lead them to Christ as their personal Savior or to strengthen their faith. CFDb is an online tool for individuals and churches to search films via titles or categories.

Join CFDb in working to change lives through Christian Films.

❖ **Tracy Briggs- Christian Book Editor**

www.rightwords.vpweb.com

Tracy Briggs is a communications and marketing professional with extensive experience writing and editing content for the web, email and direct mail marketing, B2B and medical/dental markets, as well as books, e-newsletters and magazine features.

She is a self-motivated, results driven professional who leads by positive example. She shines in a team environment, and loves building and motivating teams. She has proven strengths and training in content & creative writing, editing and collaborative problem-solving. She can be reached at briggst003@gmail.com.

We appreciate the outstanding work of the rest of the filmmakers whose clips are linked in the book:

- Igniter Media- *Strangers*
- Eastwind Productions and Provident Films Distribution- *Most/The Bridge*
- The Kendrick Brothers - (formerly Sherwood Productions) *Fireproof and Facing the Giants*
- Red Meadow Creative - *Identity*
- Paramount Pictures- *Forrest Gump*
- Brent McCorkle, Producer/Director-*Unconditional*
- The Skit Guys- *The Skinny on Prayer*
- Five & Two Pictures-*October Baby*
- Echolight Studios-*Undaunted: The Early Life of Josh McDowell*
- Ransom TV/Billy Graham Evangelistic Association - *Seklas Seeds*
- Right Now Ministries- *Work is Worship*
- Sony Pictures Animation-*Surf's Up*
- 5 Forty 2 Media Productions-*Legacy*
- Universal Pictures Illumination Entertainment- *The Lorax*
- Matthew West- *Do Something Lyric Video*

We also appreciate these other companies that helped to make this book possible.

- Godtube- Christian film streaming service
- Sermon Spice- Christian film clip service
- Wingclips- film clip service
- Xulon Press- Christian Publisher (original publisher)
- Scott Douglas and Fix This in Post- trailer company
- Desk Top Author- Enhanced E-book publishing program and service (original book version)
- Ingram Spark- Publisher 2nd Edition
- Fiverr- book cover and book formatting services

Other Books by Dr. Patty Sadallah

Journey to the Abundant Christian Life is a **thought provoking and experiential** Discipleship Bible study companion to Clips that Move Mountains that will help you:

- Take the objectives of the Clips book above to **a more personal level,**
- Incorporate the learnings with additional media, exercises and resources **to grow your faith**, and
- Become fully equipped to facilitate the 11- week Bible study in your own homes and churches if you desire.
- **Learn in community** with your home group or church class.

Dr. Patty Sadallah takes readers through their own personal journey **from worrier to warrior** and shows them how **to receive healing and direction from Jesus Himself.**

Understanding who God is, what He does, who you are as His beloved child and walking in that authority are the secrets to living a worry-free life.

Readers will **experience** the difference between **KNOWING ABOUT GOD to KNOWING HIM intimately.**

Dr. Sadallah provides encountering exercises using tools and tips for **two-way communication with God,** Biblical research tips that help identify the Names and Promises of God so readers can anchor their faith and **learn how to pray with authority.**

Look for *How to Find Your Calling: Just ask Jesus Series Book 2* coming 2019! All books are available on Amazon. Search Patty Sadallah.

End Notes

All Bible verses are from BibleGateway.com by Zondervan (2013) and are in NIV version unless otherwise noted.

1. "7 Reasons to Follow Jesus", DVD of Grace Church CMA Church service including Baptism of the Lakota family February 12, 2012

2. "Pray for Rain" video clip from *Faith Like Potatoes* film, Global Creative Studios (2006) and streamed by GodTube, http://www.godtube.com/watch/?v=WYLPGGNX

3. Impact info from biography page of Angus Buchan on his website http://www.shalomtrust.co.za/

4. *Strangers* video clip by Igniter Media and streamed by Sermon Spice, (2011) http://www.sermonspice.com/product/43168/strangers

5. Beth Moore, *The Inheritance Listening Guide* DVD Session 6 page 16-17 (2009)

6. Ibid page Session 3 page 8-9

7. *Prophetic Proof* video clip by Echoing Praise (2011)

streamed by YouTube http://www.youtube.com/watch?v=QbwwhkIP-hQ&feature=share&list=PL2A2475AB1CDF51E9

8. Mark Dunagan, *Jesus in Prophesy,* website article http://www.ch-of-christ.beaverton.or.us/Jesus_In_Prophecy.htm

9. *The Works of Henry Parry Liddon* Compilation Article by Anglican History http://anglicanhistory.org/liddon/list.html

10. Peter Stoner, *Science Speaks: Scientific Proof of the Accuracy of Prophecy and the Bible 107* (Chicago, Moody Press, 1969).

11. Dr. Cathy R. Turner, "29 Prophesies-24 hours" Blog article Leading Forward postdate March 28, 2010 http://leadingforward.blogspot.com/2010/03/29-prophecies-24-hours.html

12. Lee Strobel, the *Case for Christ: A Journalist Personal Investigation of the Evidence of Jesus* (Zondervan, 1998) page 270

13. *Lee Strobel Quotes* Goodreads website article page 1

http://www.goodreads.com/author/quotes/639.Lee_Strobel

14.   Ibid page 2

15.   27 Best Lee Strobel Quotes website article by Faith and Entertainment http://www.faithandentertainment.com/27-best-lee-strobel-quotes/

16.   Lee Strobel, the *Case for Christ: A Journalist Personal Investigation of the Evidence of Jesus* (Zondervan, 1998) page 270

17. Josh Mcdowell, *My Journey... from skepticism to faith* book, Tyndale House Publishers, (2009) page 42

18. "You Need Him" clip from *Fireproof* film, Sherwood Pictures (2008) streamed by Wingclips.com http://www.wingclips.com/movie-clips/fireproof/you-need-him

19. "The Bridge" Clip from *Most/The Bridge* film, Eastwood Productions and Provident Films (2003) and streamed by GodTube, http://www.godtube.com/

watch/?v=WYLPG7NX

20. Jonathan Schaeffer "In the Beginning"...Getting the Big Picture Know the Bible (Part 1) Sermon Notes October 7, 2012

21. "Identity" clip by Red Meadow Creative offered by Sermon Spice https://www.sermonspice.com/product/66673/identity

22. "Pray for Shrimp" clip from *Forrest Gump* film, Paramount Pictures (1994) streamed by Wingclips.com, http://www.wingclips.com/movie-clips/forrest-gump/pray-for-shrimp

23. Ray Hilbert, *Biblically Based Decision Making*, Truth at Work Curriculum training document, (2009)

24. "The Skinny on Prayer" video clip by the Skit Guys and streamed by The Skit Guys, http://skitguys.com/videos/item/the-skinny-on-prayer

25. "Trailer" clip from Unconditional film, Harbinger Media Partners, (2012) and streamed by Christian Film Database, http://www.christianfilmdatabase.com/review/unconditional/

26. Share the Love clip from *Unconditional* film, Harbinger Media Partners, (2012) and streamed by GodTube, http://www.godtube.com/watch/?v=01B21MNU

27. Brent McCorkle, Amy Parker, Rob Corley and Chuck

Vollmer *Firebird* children's book, B&H publishing Group (Oct 1, 2012)

28. Joe Bradford, About Joe Bradford website page http://www.Papajoe.org

29. "Getting to Forgiveness" clip from *October Baby* DVD, Five & 2 Pictures (2012) streamed by GodTube, http://www.godtube.com/watch/?v=WYLPYLNX

30. "Dad's Transformation" clip from *Undaunted: The Early Life of Josh McDowell* film, Echolight, (2009) streamed by GodTube, http://www.godtube.com/watch/?v=WYLPYWNX

31. Douglas Phillips and Geoffrey Botkin, *A Biblical Worldview for Film* CD disc 1, Vision Form Ministries, (2010)

32. "Nothing is Impossible" clip from *King's Faith* film, Faith Street Film Partners, streamed by GodTube, http://www.godtube.com/watch/?v=WYLPYPNX

33. "Turn it Over to God" clip from *King's Fait* film, Faith Street Film Partners, streamed by GodTube, http://www.godtube.com/watch/?v=01B2EJNU

34. "Ready Yourself to Share the Truth" clip from *Seklas Seeds* film, Ransom Tee Vee and streamed by GodTube, http://www.godtube.com/watch/?v=01B2E1NU

35. "How to Follow God's Lead" *God Speaks* video clip from Floodgate Productions and streamed by Floodgate Produc-tions, http://www.floodgateproductions.com/index.php/god-speaks.html

36. *Work is Worship* illustration clip, Right Now Ministries

and streamed by YouTube.com, http://www.youtube.com/watch?v=m06DYIAeCtU

37. Jonathan Schaeffer, "A note from Jonathan" (June, 24, 2012) Church bulletin message.

38. "Prepare Your Fields" clip from *Facing the Giants* film, Sherwood Productions (2006) and streamed from Wingclips, http://www.wingclips.com/movie-clips/facing-the-giants/prepare-your-fields

39. "Making the Board" clip from *Surf's Up* animated film and streamed from Wingclips, http://www.wingclips.com/movie-clips/surfs-up/making-the-board

40. "How will you be Remembered" *Legacy* video clip by 5 Forty 2 Media Productions, and streamed from Sermon Spice, http://www.sermonspice.com/product/1772/legacy

41. Barna Research Report, "Christians: More Like Jesus or Pharasees? Online article (April 30, 2013) https://www.barna.org/barna-update/faith-spirituality/611-christians-more-like-jesus-or-pharisees#.UfK8AYnD_IU

42. "Plant the Seed" clip from *The Lorax* animated film, Universal Pictures Illumination Entertainment (and streamed from Wingclips.com, http://www.wingclips.com/movie-clips/the-lorax/plant-the-seed

43. Matthew West, "Do Something" Lyric Video from Matthew *West Into the Light Album*, (2012) streamed from YouTube, http://www.youtube.com/watch?v=0I2csO7_pOI

44. *Your Light* video clip, James Grocho streamed by James

Grocho, http://www.jamesgrocho.com/portfolio/your-light/

45. *Our Message in 8 Minutes video* by Dr. Mark Virkler, Communion with God Ministries. Streamed from YouTube https://www.youtube.com/watch?v=8czdKN4U0hc&t=2s

www.ingramcontent.com/pod-product-compliance
Lightning Source LLC
Chambersburg PA
CBHW070731020526
44118CB00035B/1180